Schleiermacher's Preaching, Dogmatics, and Biblical Criticism

Princeton Theological Monograph Series

K. C. Hanson, Series Editor

Recent volumes in the series

Bonnie L. Pattison
Poverty in the Theology of John Calvin

Anette Ejsing
Theology of Anticipation:
A Constructive Study of C. S. Peirce

Michael G. Cartwright
Practices, Politics, and Performance:
Toward a Communal Hermeneutic for Christian Ethics

Stephen Finlan and Vladimir Kharlamov, editors
Theōsis: Deification in Christian Theology

John A. Vissers
The Neo-Orthodox Theology of W. W. Bryden

Sam Hamstra, editor
The Reformed Pastor by John Williamson Nevin

Byron C. Bangert
Consenting to God and Nature:
Toward a Theocentric, Naturalistic, Theological Ethics

Richard Valantasis et al., editors
The Subjective Eye: Essays in Honor of Margaret Miles

Caryn Riswold
Coram Deo: Human Life in the Vision of God

Schleiermacher's Preaching, Dogmatics, and Biblical Criticism

The Interpretation of Jesus Christ in the Gospel of John

Catherine L. Kelsey

Pickwick *Publications*
An imprint of *Wipf and Stock Publishers*
199 West 8th Avenue • Eugene OR 97401

SCHLEIERMACHER'S PREACHING, DOGMATICS, AND BIBLICAL CRITICISM
The Interpretation of Jesus in the Gospel of John

Princeton Theological Monograph Series 68

ISBN 10: 1-59752-905-2
ISBN 13: 978-1-59752-905-1

Cataloging-in-Publication data:

Schleiermacher's preaching, dogmatics and biblical criticism : the interpretation of Jesus in the gospel of John / Catherine L. Kelsey.

Princeton Theological Monograph Series 68

xii + 188 p ; 23 cm.

Includes bibliography

ISBN 10: 1-59752-905-2
ISBN 13: 978-1-59752-905-1

1. Schleiermacher, Friedrich, 1768–1834. 2. Schleiermacher, Friedrich, 1768–1834—Christliche Glaube. 3. Schleiermacher, Friedrich, 1768–1834—Contributions in exegesis. 4. Schleiermacher, Friedrich, 1768–1834—Contributions in preaching. I. Title. II. Series.

B3097.K45 2007

Manufactured in the U.S.A.

To my parents,
MYRON P. KELSEY AND JOAN T. KELSEY,
who have always modeled profound faith
and deep reflection on it.

Contents

Preface

It will not surprise the reader who enters very far into this work to learn that the author is both a United Methodist pastor and a theologian. I acknowledge this at the beginning because it will help the reader anticipate my attention to Schleiermacher's use of piety. He was educated as a child in the same Moravian community that John Wesley had visited fifty years earlier and that had strongly influenced Wesley's theology and preaching. Schleiermacher's integration of piety into his theology was not immediately evident to me when I first read *Christian Faith*. I trust that it will be much clearer to the reader as a result of this study. Whether or not my readers agree with my reading of Schleiermacher or with his way of relating the expression of Christian faith in practice to its critical and reflective expression in theology and biblical criticism, my goal in this work is to invite the reader to think carefully about the relationship as it currently exists and as it might exist.

This work has developed over a little more than a decade. It began as doctoral work and I am deeply indebted to Harvard Professor Richard R. Niebuhr for the conversations and careful reading and guidance he provided, particularly his attention to theological nuance both in Schleiermacher's thought and in my own. As will become clear in the second and third chapters, I am also deeply indebted to the Berlin-Brandenburgische Akademie der Wissenschaften for access to and photocopies of key portions of the Schleiermacher manuscripts in their archive. However, I would have been at a loss to make use of this resource without the assistance of the Schleiermacherforschungstelle, Berlin directed by Professor Kurt-Victor Selge. In particular, Dr. Wolfgang Virmond was very generous with his time, teaching me to read 19th century German handscript and Schleiermacher's peculiar abbreviations. He also read through with me his personal listing of all the entries in Schleiermacher's daily dairies so that we could locate as many of the occasions when Schleiermacher preached on Johannine texts as possible. This information was accessible in no other form and it made possible a much clearer picture of Schleiermacher's preaching on the Gospel of John.

Since the time this work was first developed as a dissertation a significant number of the texts referred to have appeared in the *Kritische Gesamtausgabe* and several studies related to matters discussed have appeared. Reference to these works has been incorporated into both the notes, and where appropriate, into the main text.

Chapter five will appear, reframed for a different argument, in a forthcoming edition of *New Athenaeum/ Neues Athenaeum*. I am grateful for the permission of Edwin Mellen Press for its republication.

Finally, I want to acknowledge the joy of daily conversation about Schleiermacher with my spouse, Terrence N. Tice. This work is considerably improved by his encouragement, suggestions, and the clarification that comes from our disagreements. What errors might remain are fully my responsibility.

Denver, Colorado
Advent 2006

Abbreviations

This study uses several common conventions in Schleiermacher scholarship that bear explanation. The collected works of Schleiermacher were first published in the nineteenth century in the *Sämmtliche Werke* (SW). It is structured into three divisions and each division begins anew with volume one. Works in the *Sämmtliche Werke* are conventionally referred to with a roman numeral for the major division and an arabic numeral for the volume. So the first of the two volumes containing Schleiermacher's sermons in the series on John is notated: SW II/8, which means *Sämmtliche Werke* second division, volume 8. The *Kritische Gesamtausgabe* (KGA), still in process, uses a similar three part division notated: KGA I.7,1, which designates the first half volume of the 1821/22 edition of *Der christliche Glaube.*

On Religion: Speeches to its Cultured Despisers is conventionally referred to as the *Speeches* in English and as the *Reden* in German.

Dates in the notes citing sermons follow the German practice of stating the date before the month: Date. Month. Year. A complete listing of all of the publications of works by Schleiermacher is provided by Wichmann von Meding, *Bibliographie Schleiermachers*, Schleiermacher-Archiv 9 (Berlin: Walter de Gruyter, 1992). Meding assigns a number to each of the published sermons: P (for Predigt) and a number. I have provided this number with the citations of the sermons because it allows the reader to locate other publications of the sermon, including in later printings of the *Sämmtliche Werke*, which sometimes has different pagination for the same volume. Each footnote citation of a sermon is annotated. Material in parentheses includes the biblical text for the sermon, the date on which the sermon was preached, and if published the Predigt number assigned by Meding (Pxxx).

Footnote references follow the *Chicago Manual of Style* (15th edition) convention of providing a short title. Complete references for all works are found in the Bibliography.

1

Introduction

I know of nothing better to desire for my life than the uniting of the podium and the pulpit.[1]

HE did well what could not be done today at all. He combined critical and innovative constructive scholarly work in theology, ethics, biblical studies, hermeneutics, church history, psychology, pedagogy, and philosophy with skillful pastoral leadership of a thriving congregation. Friedrich Daniel Ernst Schleiermacher was best known during his lifetime (1768–1834) as a biblical preacher of singular skill and popularity. Ten percent of the population of Berlin, twenty thousand people, lined the streets in the February cold to honor his funeral procession. He was pastor of one congregation for his entire twenty-five-years' tenure as a professor of theology in Berlin. In contrast, today Schleiermacher is best known for his writing and academic lectures. His theological writing opened the modern era in Christian theology and still provides a touchstone for systematic theology.

As Schleiermacher fully recognized, because faith is manifest only in particularity, that is, in historical human contexts, it cannot be adequately described without a considered use of the discipline of historical criticism. At issue since the rise of historical criticism is what constitutes an appropriate or considered use of it when Christian faith is being described. I begin with the assumption that we may understand the relationship between dogmatics and historical-critical biblical criticism more fully if we examine them in relation to faith's expression. The body of Schleiermacher's work allows us to think carefully about precisely those relationships if we approach his preaching as an immediate communication of his faith within

1. Dilthey, ed. *Schleiermachers Leben*, 4:176. The letter containing this statement is from Schleiermacher to a former student from Halle in 1810. Throughout this study if an English source is not named, the translation is mine.

the context of religious community—which is how he himself defined the preaching act.

The chief purpose of this study is to investigate more closely the relationship between historical-critical interpretations, dogmatic interpretations, and faith interpretations of Jesus Christ. Schleiermacher provides us with a wonderful opportunity to explore the question both in the abstract through his propositions in *Brief Outline of Theology as a Field of Study*, and in its concrete complexities through his practices of ministry and of scholarly reflection. The relationships that emerge between Schleiermacher's practices of preaching, dogmatic writing, and historical-critical biblical interpretation emphasize the interactive relations between them underlying *Brief Outline*, though, as I will show, the relations are more interactive than the linear presentation of *Brief Outline* may seem to imply.

Such an investigation is an impossibly large task, so I have narrowed it sufficiently to make it manageable. Schleiermacher quoted and alluded to the Gospel of John with some frequency in his dogmatic work. It was his favorite preaching text. And he strenuously argued for its reliability as a historical source for the life events, teachings, and thought of Jesus. Interpreters of Schleiermacher have often made use of the symbol of the Logos or Word from the prologue of the Gospel of John to characterize key aspects of Schleiermacher's Christology.[2] Such uses of a Johannine symbol with which Schleiermacher was familiar invite us to clarify how Schleiermacher himself understood and used the Johannine text.

This study will carefully investigate Schleiermacher's use and interpretation of the Gospel of John in his preaching throughout his career, in his chief dogmatic work, *Christian Faith*, and in the historical-critical judgments gathered together in his *Life of Jesus* lectures. The approach will both clarify Schleiermacher's reliance upon the Gospel of John and identify and describe key strands of the complex interrelationship between his preaching, his dogmatic work, and his historical-critical work.

I am providing a distinctive reading of Schleiermacher by doing three things in chapters two to five: by reading his preaching, his expression of piety, before all else; by inquiring into the relationship between that preaching and both his dogmatic and historical-critical work; and finally by examining how he interpreted a portion of scripture across his career and across genres. I did not entirely find what I had expected. I expected that Schleiermacher's preaching influenced his dogmatic work, and, as I

2. There are far too many instances to make listing them here useful. One of the most recent is the monograph by DeVries, *Jesus Christ in the Preaching of Calvin and Schleiermacher.*

shall show, it did so significantly. I also expected that his preaching directly influenced his historical-critical judgments. It now appears to me that it did not do so directly. I provide a reading of Schleiermacher as a critical historian and describe the indirect influence on historical judgments exerted by the selection of historical-critical criteria.

I will not attempt to argue for this reading in opposition to the countless others which have gone before, though from time to time I will note specific disagreements in footnotes. The reading will speak for itself in its fruitfulness for you, the reader, particularly if it invites you to return to Schleiermacher's texts themselves with new questions to consider.

The Theoretical Relationship between Dogmatics, Biblical Criticism, and Preaching

Schleiermacher's *Brief Outline of Theology as a Field of Study* provides an organization and a rationale for a scholarly approach to reflection upon Christianity.[3] The published work appeared in the form of propositions without elaboration in its first edition in 1811. The propositions functioned as the beginning points for Schleiermacher's lectures on the subject.[4] The second, revised edition appeared in 1830 and included a brief elaboration of the ideas under each proposition. It was a course important to Schleiermacher; the only other lectures he offered so frequently were on dogmatics and Christian ethics.

Brief Outline is carefully designed to emphasize simultaneously and equally two perspectives on Christianity. The first is *Wissenschaft*, careful critical study yielding a knowledge that comes as close to the truth as human effort can get. The second is religious interest, the lived faith of persons who are aware of their intimate relationship with God. The two do not conflict but necessarily coincide for Schleiermacher, because truth is associated with God. In fact, the two provide balance and a check against

3. *Kurze Darstellung, 1977*; trans. Tice, *Brief Outline.*

4. By the time of its first publication Schleiermacher had lectured on theological encyclopedia (the German term for the organization of theological study) three times in its entirety (Winter 1804/05, Summer 1805, Winter 1808) and had begun the lectures twice more in the Fall of 1806, interrupted by the occupation of Halle, and in the Winter term 1810/11, during which the published work appeared. Schleiermacher had lectured on theological encyclopedia another seven times before publishing the second edition. After the appearance of the second edition he repeated the lectures one final time, for a total of twelve complete sets of lectures during his thirty years of teaching. See Scholz, "Einleitung" in *Kurze Darstellung,* xii–xvi.

the distortion that is possible when either perspective is taken alone. The question, then, is *how* these two complement and correct one another.

One significant way in which this complementarity is manifest is in the relationship between theological interest in the narrow sense of *Wissenschaft* and church leadership. This axis between the role of a theologian and the role of a clergyperson runs through the entire work. The relationship between them is described in ideal terms with reference to a "prince of the church"—a person in whom there is balance between both religious interest and scholarly interest for the purpose of both practical and theoretical activity.[5] This is not simply a rarely achieved ideal, however. Theology that is pursued without engaging church interest is no longer theological, and church leadership that is acting without the knowledge gained through *Wissenschaft* is only confused action.[6] Thus, neither activity is fully itself without the simultaneous engagement of the other. This is true even of historical study. "Nothing is more fruitless than a piling up of historical learning which neither serves any practical purpose nor offers anything for the use of others in its presentation."[7] On the other hand, religious interest that is stripped of *Wissenschaft* cannot give true results and can only reflect the subjectivity of the person or the party to which the person belongs.[8] The unity of scholarly interest and religious interest is again emphasized in the definition of practical theology. Practical theology is a unification of these two.[9]

Schleiermacher did not himself work through all the complexities of the problem of the relationship between faith and history. As long as he had what he considered eyewitness access to the historical Jesus, it was possible to define Christianity as the field lying between historical research into Jesus and expressions of living faith, the field lying between cause and effect. Since Schleiermacher historical research has generally concluded that we cannot gain direct access to the cause, Jesus, through the sources available; we only have access to records created as effects. This leaves historical research arguing from effect to probable cause.

The word "fact," as Schleiermacher used it, denotes a historical construction. He viewed the recording of spatial and temporal changes as a mechanical operation, but the determination of a fact involves a historical apprehension (*Anschauung*) in which the outer physical reality and the

5. *Kurze Darstellung*, §9, 3–4; trans., Tice, 5–6.
6. Ibid., §12, 5; trans., Tice, 8.
7. Ibid., §191, 72; trans., Tice, 95.
8. Ibid., §248, 94; trans., Tice, 124.
9. Ibid., §258, 99; trans., Tice, 131.

inner soul are combined into one coherent perception. This means that although several persons have noticed exactly the same physical events, they may interpret the fact of those events very differently.[10] A history is constructed of facts as just defined, that is, with an interpretation which brings together external changes and inner unity into one consistent perception. Only in this way is history able to be useful to church leadership. It is the interpretation of external changes in light of some unifying principle that provides a basis for judgments about what is healthy diversity and what is schismatic or diseased. A chronicle of changes that treats all events equally and in sequence is neither a history nor a theological activity.[11] A true historical account has double vision. It sees moments in their individuality and peculiar relationships, and it sees those same moments as part of an infinite continuity of development of an identifiable impulse.[12]

There are three aspects to the verification of doctrinal propositions in the 1830 edition of *Brief Outline*. The first is consistency with the biblical canon. The second is consistency with other propositions in the doctrinal system. The third is a condition of verification, that is, lived belief in the doctrine. The first two aspects are functions of rigorous scholarship. The third results from the definition of what is dogmatic or doctrinal. That is, propositions are only of historical interest if they are believed. Convincing demonstration of the truth of propositions results, by definition, in belief in the truth of the propositions. Thus, we may treat as doctrine only that which is true for us.[13] Other systems of belief, even within the Evangelical Church, are of historical interest but not of doctrinal interest.

Schleiermacher divided theology into three parts: philosophical theology, historical theology, and practical theology. Since theology as a whole is defined by Schleiermacher as a positive science the aim of which is to assist in the leadership of the Christian church, it is fitting that the first edition of *Brief Outline* names practical theology "the crown of theology."[14] This implies a movement that is immediately made explicit in the propositions that follow: historical theology requires the agency of philosophical theology in order adequately to inform practical theology.[15] Employment of the logical ordering is hindered, according to Schleiermacher, by the inadequate development of philosophical theology, nevertheless the move-

10. Ibid., §§151–2, 59; trans., Tice, 79.

11. Ibid., §153, 60; trans., Tice, 79–80.

12. Ibid., §150, 58–9; trans., Tice, 78–9.

13. Ibid., §98, 41–2; trans., Tice, 56, §§195–196, 73–4; trans., Tice, 97–100, §204, 78; trans., Tice, 103–4, §249, 95; trans., Tice, 125–6.

14. Ibid., I §31, 10; trans., Tice, 15.

15. Ibid., §30, 12; trans., Tice, 18.

ment is clear—philosophical theology to historical theology to practical theology. On the other hand, this clear linear progression is accompanied by Schleiermacher's observation that "historical theology is the actual corpus of theological study, which corpus is connected with science, as such, by means of philosophical theology and with the active Christian life by means of practical theology."[16] This statement implies an interactive relationship between the parts of theology. Interaction is also implied by Schleiermacher's insistence that anyone who deals with one of the theological disciplines must have mastery of the basic aspects of each of the disciplines.[17] So we find two tendencies at work in Schleiermacher's description in *Brief Outline*: a linear progression from philosophical theology to historical theology to practical theology, and an interactive tendency that treats the disciplines as interrelated.

Historical-critical biblical research and dogmatics both belong to historical theology. Dogmatics is the systematic presentation of faith that has currency at a given time in the Christian church or, in times of division, in one part of it.[18] However, to understand fully what is believed in the present one must understand how it has developed out of what has come before. This requires a discipline of historical theology. Schleiermacher gave preeminence to the original expression of Christian faith, because it has the least variation in its expression and so provides us with the purest form of the unity and distinctive nature of Christianity. For this reason, it is studied first within historical theology, and dogmatics (including doctrine and ethics), which makes a direct transition into practical theology, is studied last.[19] Note that Schleiermacher thereby made the New Testament an important arbiter of Christian faith without giving it the exclusive authority it would hold if it were in itself divine revelation. The authority Schleiermacher gave to the New Testament also requires the use of historical criticism in order to discern and appropriate what is essential to Christianity. Within Schleiermacher's description of historical theology there are tendencies toward linear progression: from exegetical theology to historical theology to dogmatic theology. Moreover, there are reminders that the disciplines interact and overlap: such as the admission that "primitive Christianity is also included within the total career of Christianity."[20]

16. Ibid., §28, 11–2; trans., Tice, 17.
17. Ibid., §16, 6; trans., Tice, 10.
18. Ibid., §97, 41; trans., Tice, 54–5.
19. Ibid., §82–5, 35–36; trans., Tice, 47–9.
20. Ibid., §84, 36; trans., Tice, 48.

In *Brief Outline* preaching is addressed as being not simply a part of practical theology but as being an aspect of it contingent on historical context.[21] Christian worship is described as an enduring aspect of the art of communicating religious self-consciousness; but preaching, whether in homilies or sermons, is described as something resulting from the development of the Evangelical church.[22] Preaching is firmly subordinated to the larger context of common worship. In this position it is limited, as is common worship, to expressing "notions which also have their place within the body of Church doctrine."[23] Thus, it would appear that a linear progression from historical-critical biblical exegesis to dogmatics to preaching is prescribed here for the practice of the church. A hint that this clear progression might be more interactive is given in Schleiermacher's definition of what makes Christian worship effective or edifying: It depends upon the communication of that pious self-consciousness which has come into thought.[24] It is this same pious, Christian self-consciousness that is thematized by dogmatics.

So, *Brief Outline* leaves us asking whether dogmatic theology might both end in preaching *and* begin with preaching because preaching is an expression of pious, Christian self-consciousness. Further, if dogmatic theology does begin and end in preaching, then what is the role of the biblical text and historical-critical interpretation of it in relation to that preaching and dogmatics? These questions are premised upon a linear reading of the relationship between biblical criticism, dogmatics, and preaching, a linear reading which is contra-indicated at a few points in the text itself. As I shall show in the following chapters, an examination of Schleiermacher's own practices of biblical criticism, dogmatics, and preaching suggest that we should read the relationships described in *Brief Outline* as being more interactive than linear.

The Plan for This Study

The plan for the presentations that follow proceeds in four steps. Chapter two provides a picture of the complex historical contexts in which Schleiermacher preached and of the difficulties inherent in the written sources for his preaching, and it concludes by providing a model for addressing his preaching on John as a body of work. The third chapter employs this mod-

21. Ibid., §284, 109–110; trans., Tice, 145.
22. Ibid., §280, 108; trans., Tice, 143, and §284, 110; trans., Tice, 145.
23. Ibid., §281, 108; trans., Tice, 144.
24. Ibid., §280, 108; trans., Tice, 143.

el by examining the important texts in Schleiermacher's preaching on John and identifying three key presuppositions at work in all of that preaching, across both his career as a preacher and the texts themselves. The fourth chapter then turns to *Christian Faith* and describes three significant strands of relationship between that text and Schleiermacher's preaching on John. The fifth chapter describes the work of Schleiermacher in his *Life of Jesus* lectures as an historian and as an exegete of the Gospel of John, and it interprets the relationship between Schleiermacher's preaching presuppositions and his historical-critical criteria. The conclusion considers implications of this study for Schleiermacher scholarship in particular and the study of theology in general.

We begin, then, with an introduction to the preaching of the most significant preacher of his generation in central Europe.

2

An Introduction to Schleiermacher's Preaching and the Difficulties It Presents

In his remembrance published soon after Schleiermacher's death in 1834, Friedrich Lücke provided this description of his teacher and friend's preaching:

> Whoever experienced it, noticed how the artistry of the Christian discourse grew, how it slowly and quietly at the beginning, more in ordinary tone of speech, collected and ordered the thoughts; then, however, when he had spoken for a bit and he had both extended and tightened the entire net of thoughts, the speech became quicker, more excited, and the nearer to the hortatory or encouraging closure, the more flowing and rich.[1]

Lücke was describing the style of preaching which Schleiermacher had developed over his preaching career of forty years. The style was distinctive in itself, and it was different from what educated listeners anticipated because of its modesty and lack of ornamentation.[2] One of the features upon which his contemporaries often remarked was Schleiermacher's practice of preaching without having written out the sermon completely in advance. With only an outline in front of him, his attention was directed entirely to the congregation before him, suggesting that his development of the points of the sermon might respond to nonverbal feedback as he preached.

Preaching is an event encompassing more than a sermon text. It is easy when one is reading sermon texts to treat them as one would any other text and to lose sight of the fact that they are, at best, partial representations of complex events that have occurred in particular places at

1. Lücke, "Erinnerungen," 789.
2. Blackwell, "Martensen's 'Bekenntnis zu Schleiermacher,'" 8.

specific moments. Unlike printed material, which can be re-read and compared to other texts directly, preaching unfolds sequentially and is fleeting. What endures and allows comparison is entirely a function of memory, the memory of the speaker or the memory of listeners. This is true of sermons that are written out entirely in advance, because the speaking involves voice inflection, gestures, pauses, and changes in the written text, none of which can be conveyed by the written text. It is even more true of preaching delivered without a manuscript. We are dependent upon memory, with all of its filters, for access to Schleiermacher's preaching.

In order to compare it to his other work, when considering Schleiermacher's preaching as a whole, we need to attend to that which characterizes the whole. In the process of introducing the sermons, this chapter will sketch three factors that make such characterizations difficult: the variety of contexts, both historical and ecclesial, within which Schleiermacher preached; the nature of the sources for the sermons; and the development that can be traced across Schleiermacher's preaching career.

Historical Contexts for Schleiermacher's Preaching

The contexts in which Schleiermacher preached have twofold significance. They are a part of the preaching event, though often not directly acknowledged in the written representation of it. Moreover, contexts influence the attention to and memory of what is said; context makes some statements more memorable than others. What is memorable in context goes into a listener's later account of preaching more readily than what is less interesting in context. Because Schleiermacher was considered a memorable preacher, we may reasonably expect that he was conscious of and responsive to the contexts in which he was preaching.

What is important to note first is the variety of contexts in which Schleiermacher preached. These contexts are distinguished both by enormous socio-political changes across the more than forty years of preaching and by fundamentally different circumstances in which persons gathered for worship in Schleiermacher's various preaching assignments.

This is not the place for a history of Prussia between 1790 and 1834, nor for a biography of Schleiermacher.[3] However, Schleiermacher's preaching cannot be appreciated on the basis of the texts that record it

3. See Sheehan, *German History 1770–1866*, for a masterful history in English the documentation of which is an excellent introduction to the primary literature that reveals the social and political life of the period. Dilthey's *Leben Schleiermachers* is now surpassed in accuracy as the definitive biographical account by Nowak's *Schleiermacher*. A brief account of Schleiermacher's life in English can be found in chapter one, Tice, *Schleiermacher*, 1–18.

without the reader's being aware of the contexts of that preaching. A brief sketch of the events of the period and then of the congregations to which Schleiermacher preached will serve to bring the contexts into view.

When Schleiermacher delivered his first sermons in the very late 1780s the French Revolution had just begun. The ideals of the Revolution soon turned to excesses. As word of the Revolution traveled in the German lands, including Prussia, the ideals spawned considerable intellectual conversation about how those ideals might be realized in German contexts. These conversations evoked political reaction, mostly negative, which intensified as word of the developing excesses of the French Revolution spread. Because Enlightenment ideas were viewed as the ideology of revolution, the 1790s in Prussia saw increasing censorship of publications regarded by those in authority as promoting the Enlightenment.[4] New ideas were perceived to threaten the political order, an order that included religious institutions. The tension between order and established authority, on the one hand, and expression and discussion of alternative ideals, on the other, is a constant in the Prussian public life of this period. It is present both in attempted political reforms and in strong backlash and censure.

The period of Schleiermacher's young and middle adulthood was marked by constantly shifting political alliances between nations and within Prussia in response to French military activity. France defeated Prussia in 1793–94. Prussia held to neutrality between 1795 and 1806 and then was badly defeated and occupied by France in 1806–07. From 1807 until 1813 Prussia functioned as a junior partner under French hegemony. All of these circumstances made political and economic reform unavoidable if Prussia were to survive. It was not until agreements were made in Vienna in 1815 that the political situation stabilized. From 1793 to 1815 large amounts of German-speaking territory changed hands and many independent political units permanently disappeared. Within Prussia the major public institutions, military, bureaucratic, and economic, underwent significant if guarded reform.[5] Feudal relations were irrevocably dissolved, though without making substantial changes in the distribution of power between classes. The dissolution of feudal structures made possible the movement of workers and the transfers of land and asset ownership required for industrialization to occur.

4. Demps, et.al., *Geschichte Berlins,* 301.

5. Sheehan sees that reform as the important legacy of this period to later German history. In his view it is more influential than the various rhetorics of nationalism that emerged in response to French military successes.

In James Sheehan's description, German response to revolution in the French mode (liberty, equality, fraternity) is not so much backlash as an extension of moral reform into educational, social, political, and artistic life. The state was idealized as a moral community and thus a source of strength. Moreover, this community was politicized as semi-authoritarian, because that form was deemed to be the most stable and to maintain the privilege of the educated. The rhetoric of the German *Volk* (people), which was useful in fighting the French, was taken to be a threat once Napoleon was defeated, until the Prussian government was sufficiently strong to use a conceptualization of *Volk* as an ideal with which to promulgate unity under Prussian dominance of German lands.

Because it was the capital city, Berlin was the center stage for these forces in Prussia. With 172,122 residents in 1800, Berlin was the sixth largest city in Europe.[6] The largest group of residents was comprised of children and youth, more than 35% of the population. (In 1789, 36% of the French population was under age 20.)[7] A large portion of these youth died between 1813 and 1815 in the fighting that liberated Berlin and freed Prussia from French influence. Berlin's major economic force was the textile industry, which involved almost one quarter of the population in some aspect of textile manufacture.[8] The pay of manufacturing workers was so low that husband, wife, and children all had to work to provide sufficient income for a family of four. The pay of handworkers remained constant between 1750 and 1800, while the cost of living had more than doubled.[9] Persons poor enough to receive public assistance constituted a third major group, more than 8% of the populace. Another large grouping in the city's population was military personnel and their families. In 1803 they were about 14% of the city's residents.[10]

In the 1790s about 1,000 Berliners earned their living as writers, academics, artists, and the like.[11] These intellectuals gathered socially in carefully cultivated salons that fostered artistic, speculative, and political discourse across disciplinary and religious (but not class) boundaries.[12]

6. Ribbe, *Geschichte Berlins,* 1:413.

7. Ibid., 1:416.

8. Demps, et.al., *Geschichte Berlins*, 297.

9. Ribbe, *Geschichte Berlins*, 1:419.

10. Ibid., 1:415.

11. Demps, et.al., *Geschichte Berlins*, 300.

12. Herz, *Berliner Salon*. This is a primary source recently published; Herz was a close friend of Schleiermacher's. For an analysis of Schleiermacher's own understanding of salon life, see Foley, *Essay on a Theory*. For more general historical studies see Wilhelmy, *Der Berliner Salon* and Hildebrandt, *Zwischen Suppenküche und Salon*.

They were the primary force behind efforts to reform the Prussian bureaucracy from an organization that bestowed and protected privilege to an organization in which effective performance of duties was the measure for advancement. In this context, calls for democracy were calls for a loosening of exclusive aristocratic power to include the educated; a profound distrust for "the mob" continued to separate the educated from workers.

Although intellectual and political tensions in Berlin were high throughout the closing decade of the 18th century and the opening years of the 19th century, daily life for the entire populace was first transformed in 1806 by the French defeat of Prussian forces at Jena. French troops entered Halle and immediately closed the university—the pride of Prussia. When it reopened within the year, Halle was the crown jewel of another land's crown. Prussia had lost vast territory. Berlin itself was an occupied city from October 24, 1806, until more than a year after the Treaty of Tilset was signed. The French garrison in Berlin did not leave until December 1808, five months after Schleiermacher had received a vocation to the Trinity Church and had begun the grace year that preceded his installation in June 1809. Since officers of the 10,000 French troops were quartered among the populace, the movements of the French army changed daily life significantly.

Berlin housed French troops again in 1812 while Prussia fulfilled treaty obligations to assist the French in their war against Russia. In early 1813, the Prussian king left Berlin and changed sides, committing Prussia to assist Russia against the French. In one night French troops marched out the Hällesches Tor (at the south end of Schleiermacher's parish and a 10 minute walk from the church building) while Russian troops marched in on the north side of the city. Later in the summer, two battles for the control of Berlin occurred at the Hällesches Tor. Berlin marked its emancipation from the French by the Prussian victory in those battles.

From the beginning of the French occupation in 1806, the economy of Berlin was severely stressed by the indemnities and expenses of quartering the troops. Taxes were constantly being raised. The publisher and bookseller Friedrich Nicolai was typical of people in business: he lost half of his personal wealth in the 20 months between November 1806 and July 1808.[13] Also, the wealthy paid less of their share of the taxes than did the tradespeople. Loans were taken out by the city that indebted it for the next sixty years, until 1867.[14] The prohibition of imports and exports to England destroyed commerce. Businesses that supplied the army survived,

13. Ribbe, *Geschichte Berlins,* 1:450.

14. Demps, et.al., *Geschichte Berlins*, 306.

while businesses that dealt with luxuries did not. Wilhelm von Humboldt described Berlin in January 1809 as having become a village with few wagons or carriages, so that even well-dressed men walked in the streets rather than rode.[15] The city to which Schleiermacher preached in his early years at Trinity Church was virtually bankrupt and severely stressed. Its residents lived in hardship and with great uncertainty.

From this low point, Berlin recovered in a period of enormous population increase and slower economic growth. The population increased 65% between 1809 and 1816 and had more than doubled by the time of Schleiermacher's death in 1834.[16] As the largest city in Prussia, Berlin attracted peasants, who had been released from the land by the October Edict of 1807, to jobs created by the beginning of Prussian industrialization. During the war years, Berlin also attracted Prussians displaced by the French redistribution of German lands, which had significantly shrunk Prussian territory. Schleiermacher's move from Halle to Berlin in 1807 is one example of this latter population movement.

The period of French occupation saw several legal changes that endured after the war period. The October Edict of 1807 changed feudal restrictions on trade, industry, real estate, and the freedom of workers to move.[17] These changes made possible capitalist industrial development and accelerated the industrialization of the city in the years following emancipation from the French. They also led to and allowed greater unemployment among skilled workers. In the reorganization of city government the police became the most significant bureaucracy, holding responsibility for oversight of security, political activities, sanitation, canals, and hygiene.[18] This leading role of the police in civic affairs continued throughout Schleiermacher's lifetime.

Until aristocratic power was reasserted following emancipation in 1813, considerable political reform was discussed and initiated. Although Schleiermacher participated in these activities, an account of his participation is beyond the scope of this study. The perception by governmental authorities of his role, as it was viewed during the period of backlash and reconsolidation of power, created a climate of suspicion and scrutiny of his public and private speech. One important aspect of the context in which Schleiermacher began preaching his series of sermons on the Gospel of John was the general accusation that he spoke inappropriately and perhaps

15. Ribbe, *Geschichte Berlins*, 1:442.

16. Figures calculated from information given by Ribbe, *Geschichte Berlins*, 1:444.

17. Demps, et.al., *Geschichte Berlins*, 307.

18. Ibid., 322.

illegally on political topics in his lectures, preaching, and correspondence. In January 1823 he spent three days explaining to the police the meaning of portions of his private correspondence from 1813, 1818, 1819, and 1823.[19] The investigation was finally resolved sometime after July 1823 in favor of Schleiermacher, allowing him to retain his positions at the University and Trinity Church. One of the arguments made in his support was that his preaching did not in any way contain political ideas.[20] The political sermons of 1806–1813 were only conceivable or deliverable in that short period of time when it was in the interest of the king to arouse broad public identification with the nation state.[21] It should not surprise the reader of the series of sermons on John, begun in 1823, that these sermons avoid political themes.

As the John series and the political sermons illustrate by their contrast with one another, Schleiermacher's preaching responded to its historical context. Enormous changes marked that context across the life of his preaching career. This makes it very difficult to characterize his preaching as a whole, except by obscuring the particularity of its historical location and treating preaching as if it were a published text. This particularity includes the congregations that gathered before him.

Church Contexts for Schleiermacher's Preaching

Schleiermacher was called to preach in five very different on-going situations over the course of his career, not including a number of guest preaching occasions. The nature of the congregations, their relationships to their communities and the communities themselves, varied greatly from each another. Each of these factors, in addition to the historical events of the period in which Schleiermacher was serving in each location, form the church contexts of Schleiermacher's preaching.

Landsberg an der Warthe was Schleiermacher's first employment as an ordained minister. He began in April 1794 as an associate to his relative, Schumann, whose health was failing. Landsberg was a small community compared to Berlin but large for a Landstadt (roughly comparable

19. Transcripts of the police report may be found in Rachold, *Friedrich Schleiermacher-eine Briefauswahl.*

20. "Altenstein und Schuckmann an den König" in ibid., 350.

21. For a thorough examination of these sermons see Bauer, *Schleiermacher als patriotischer Prediger.* For a thorough analysis of Schleiermacher's political activities across his lifetime see Wolfes, *Öffentlichkeit und Bürgergesellschaft.* An overview in English can be found in Vial, "Schleiermacher and the State." Schleiermacher's notes and student notes of his lectures on the state are published in KGA II/8, *Vorlesungen über die Lehre vom Staat.*

to an American county seat); six years after his arrival the city numbered 6,000 residents.[22] It was a city in which relationships of aristocratic privilege and obligation could still predominate. It was the administrative center for the region. The commerce of the city, particularly the manufacture of wool, was encouraged by the Prussian ruling family, the Hohenzollern. This manufacture was not yet industrialized and was largely home work.[23] Although but few details are available about the Reformed parish, there are clues. It was important enough that Schleiermacher (at age 27) was considered too young to become the pastor upon the death of Schumann. Schleiermacher's activities included not only preaching and catechizing but also tutoring. In comparing his duties in Landsberg with those of his colleagues in other parishes, this may have been his most "normal" employment as a pastor.

Schleiermacher's next assignment was a chaplaincy—very different from an assignment to a parish. His tenure in the Reformed chaplaincy at the Charité Hospital just outside the gates of Berlin began in September 1796 and, in spite of the offer of a regular congregation in one of the Landstädte, continued until 1802. Schleiermacher's responsibility was to both the hospital and the poor house at Charité and included not only preaching but also moral instruction and a full panoply of pastoral activities.[24] The appointment of the Reformed and Lutheran pastors there was jointly made by the Prussian directorates for the poor and for the church. Preaching duties were shared by the two pastors. Services were held in the Charité church in the morning and afternoon on each Sunday and festival day and on the following morning. There were also regular preaching obligations in the hospital.

After a 1798 fire destroyed the insane asylum located in Friedrichsstadt, Charité also became the mental hospital.[25] Death was a constant companion to Charité patients. Figures vary, but in this time period the death rate was between 12% and 25%.[26] In 1798 the respected Lutheran preacher for Charité, Wilhelm Prahmer, wrote a pamphlet detailing significant shortcomings in the nursing, food, and cleanliness of Charité. He charged that measures ordered by doctors were denied by administrators. His pamphlet resulted both in controversy and in some reforms and increased monetary

22. Beske and Handke, *Landsberg*, 27.

23. Ibid., 26.

24. Nowak, "Prediger am Charité," 402. This article is more detailed and more accurate in its description of this appointment than Dilthey in *Leben Schleiermachers*.

25. Jaeckel, *Charité*, 155–56.

26. Ibid., 154.

support from the crown for the chronically financially-troubled institution.[27] An enlargement of the hospital begun in 1785 and, delayed by lack of finances, was finally completed in 1800.

In 1799 Schleiermacher and his colleague, Prahmer, argued together in writing for a common liturgy among eight reforms they proposed to improve the effectiveness of the ministry at Charité.[28] This early concern for a common liturgy later helped to recommend him for the extraordinary Reformed position on the Lutheran faculty at Halle and then for the rare dual-tradition Trinity Church in Berlin.

Schleiermacher was attentive to the situation of the indigent at Charité; a brief set of fragments among his papers from this period is entitled "Concerning the Situation of the Poor" (ca. 1798).[29] The social and economic condition of the "souls" for whom Schleiermacher was responsible was marginal, and his preaching to them responded to this fact.[30] He noted in the first collection of his sermons, published in 1801, that none came from his preaching at Charité because his hearers there brought needs different from those of persons in other churches.[31]

In 1802 assignment to the position of *Hofprediger* (court chaplain) in Stolpe took Schleiermacher far from Berlin to the northern coast, but it did not return him to preaching in a normal Reformed parish. Stolpe was an early participant in the Lutheran Reformation, and the city and city church were Lutheran. The Reformed community was a tiny minority of about 50 families, consisting mostly of public servants sent to Stolpe because it was an administrative center.[32] The Schloß church in which the Reformed congregation met and in which Schleiermacher preached was a long, tall and narrow gothic structure built in the 14th and 15th centuries as the sanctuary of a Dominican monastery, which was taken over in 1602 as the church of the ruling family.[33] Until the late 17th century Stolpe was the home of the widows of the Pommeranian dynasty. It then

27. Ibid., 152–55.

28. Nowak, "Prediger am Charité," 403.

29. SN 227 "Zum Armen Wesen" in Akademie der Wissenschaften, Berlin, noted by Nowak, "Prediger an Charité," 403, and later included in KGA I/2:159–61.

30. Nowak also argues that the appointment to Charité itself was beneath the aspirations of a young man who wanted to rise in social rank and opportunity. Thus, in Nowak's reading the appointment kept Schleiermacher himself marginal socially. "Prediger am Charité," 392–97.

31. This volume was reprinted as a part of SW II/1. The reference is on p. 7.

32. Dilthey, *Leben Schleiermachers*, vol. 1, part 2, 20.

33. This is the only structure in which Schleiermacher preached regularly that remains standing.

became part of the Hohenzollern lands.[34] Stolpe contained an important military garrison and was a center for commerce because its river harbor had access to the Ostsee. It was far from the literary culture of Berlin, both in distance and in inclination, and it offered little opportunity to teach, even catechetically; Reformed children attended the Lutheran catechism. The lack of congregational cohesion and numbers likely created a discouraging setting in which to preach. Manuscript notations suggest that Schleiermacher reused sermon outlines from Landsberg for some of his preaching in Stolpe.[35]

On the fourteenth of August, 1804, Friedrich Wilhelm III, in a cabinet order, initiated academic worship services at his flagship university in Halle. This order was part of a pattern of creating social cohesion and reform through efforts at moral improvement. That it should be located at an university was a response to the pressure among intellectuals for political change. The order expected services to begin in October 1804 and made the service the responsibility of the Halle seminary faculty.[36] Schleiermacher was named extra-ordinary professor and university preacher. Due to difficulties with the faculty and various civil authorities, services did not actually begin until August 1806. The university was closed by French invasion in October of the same year. In the two months in between, Schleiermacher preached to the university and academic community in Halle—more than 1,000 of the 13,000 residents of the city.[37] Because of the historical and social context, the group of sermons that scholars call the "political" sermons began here.[38] Halle in 1804 to 1806 can best be described by contrasts: the beauty of the many private gardens with bread riots in the marketplace in 1805;[39] the color and excitement of university students with the painted gallows for deserted soldiers at one city gate; the variety of great minds, timeless and timely ideas gathered by the university with the dominance of brute physical power and social collapse under the

34. Vollack, *Hinterpommern*, 113–15.

35. SN 51 (Schleiermacher Nachlass item #51 in the Akademie der Wissenschaften, Berlin) is a manuscript the title page of which identifies the sermon outlines contained in it as being from Landsberg. Each sermon on the first pages is dated in 1802, when Schleiermacher was in Stolpe. Later sections of the manuscript are dated 1795 and 1796. The simplest explanation is that the manuscript was written during his Stolpe assignment, by copying outlines from the Landsberg period.

36. Hoffbauer, *Universität zu Halle*, 508–12.

37. Dilthey, *Leben Schleiermachers* vol. 1, part 2, 98. Contrast this high percentage to the less than 1% of Berlin's population that were students in the 1830s.

38. See Bauer, *Schleiermacher als patriotischer Prediger*.

39. Herzberg, *Geschichte der Stadt Halle*, 317.

threat of, and eventual, Napoleonic invasion. This is a far different context from any in which Schleiermacher had preached earlier. The opportunity to preach did not last long. In 1807 Schleiermacher returned to Berlin, where he was to remain except for travel until his life's end.

The context for Schleiermacher's preaching about which we know the most was his 25-year pastorate at the Trinity Church in Berlin (*Dreifaltigkeitskirche*), to which he received a call in 1808. It was located in Friedrichsstadt, one of the two largest and fastest growing districts in the city. The church's parish was bounded by the city wall on the west (located approximately where the Berlin wall stood until 1989), Hällisches Tor on the south, Friedrichsstrasse on the east, and the Behrenstrasse on the north, one block south of Unter den Linden.[40] (Parish boundaries, however, did not apply to the Reformed congregation at Trinity Church until the Reformed church and Lutheran church were united in 1822.) Approximately 40,000 people lived in Friedrichsstadt, of which the parish comprised the western third. Friedrichsstadt included a variety of housing, tradesworks, and small industry (such as a machine shop). The parish did not include any of the large public structures built during Schleiermacher's pastorate to represent Prussian power and culture, but all are within a 10-minute walk of the parish, as is the university.

Trinity Church was built by the crown as part of the development of Friedrichsstadt in the 18th Century, and the king retained the right to name its pastors. It had two congregations and two pastors—Reformed and Lutheran. When Friedrich Wilhelm III decided to unite the Reformed and Lutheran traditions into one Prussian church, Trinity Church was led by its pastors to embrace the union. In 1822 it was the first church to complete the unification process. This did not mean, however, that Schleiermacher willingly embraced the liturgy promulgated as an expression of Protestant unity.[41] He resisted the imposition of the liturgy *(Agenda)* upon congregations, not least since the liturgy in question was, in his view, largely a return to early Lutheran practices.[42]

40. Reich, *Schleiermacher als Pfarrer,* 7–8.

41. See Reich, *Schleiermacher als Pfarrer* for a description of the events occurring as a result of Schleiermacher's opposition to the liturgy. See also Nowak, *Schleiermacher*, 385–90.

42. For a study of Schleiermacher's theory of liturgy, see Albrecht, *Schleiermacher's Liturgik*. In spite of the title, this work emphasizes theory. A brief but detailed discussion of Schleiermacher's theory of liturgy and worship, using his Christian Ethics lectures and Practical Theology lectures, can be found in Schmidt, *Lied-Kirchenmusik-Predigt*, 9–18. Summary of the events of the debate about the Prussian evangelical liturgy is found in Reich, *Schleiermacher als Pfarrer*.

The Trinity Church building had a total occupancy of 1,650 persons on the ground floor and three choirs. Almost one third of these were standing places.[43] The church was regularly full for the main service. Noise was often a problem, which made hearing difficult. Eventually Schleiermacher requested that the street doors be closed during the sermon in order to minimize the intrusion of street noise, particularly the clatter of loaded wagons on the stone pavements. This context had direct implications not only for the delivery but also for the content of preaching. Content could not be dependent upon small details that were stated only once; such details were too easily lost. This limited the role of complexity in a sermon. Complexity may have served to reinforce a more general impression, but the preacher could not expect most of the congregation to hear, follow, or remember the details. Since the object of worship, as Schleiermacher conceived it, was to strengthen the listener rather than to instruct him or her,[44] complex concepts need not have been avoided, but they had to have been skillfully used toward an end beyond the concepts themselves.

The influence of congregational context on Schleiermacher's preaching is particularly evident in a comparison of two sermon outlines for sermons preached on the same text on the same day in two different congregations. On April 20, 1800, Schleiermacher preached on John 21:15 at the Werdersche Church in Berlin in the morning and at the Charité in the afternoon.[45] The main question in both sermons is self-examination: We appropriately search our hearts to evaluate ourselves, rather than comparing ourselves to others. The morning sermon, however, is more complex; it turns at the close from the question of how we evaluate our love to the question of how to love Christ directly. The afternoon sermon, preached to a less sophisticated congregation, does not make this turn and never attempts to discuss motivation for love. The content is clearly shaped in response to the congregational context.

43. Reich, *Schleiermacher als Pfarrer*, 119–20. This building was badly damaged during World War II bombing and was eventually razed.

44. *Praktische Theologie*, 215.

45. SN 53 (Akademie der Wissenschaften, Berlin), 27 and Zimmer, *aus 1800,* 43–45 (John 21:15 20.4.1800 P531); SN 53 (Akademie der Wissenschaften, Berlin), 28 and Zimmer, *aus 1800,* 45–46 (John 21:15 20.4.1800 P532). Both of these outlines are accurate as published.

Liturgical Contexts for Schleiermacher's Preaching

The narrowest aspect of the context for preaching is the worship service in which the preaching occurs. Trinity Church had three Sunday services and one Saturday evening service, the latter devoted especially to preparation for communion. The early morning service and main service rotated in leadership back and forth between the Reformed pastor and the Lutheran pastor, both before and after the union of the Reformed and Lutheran congregations of Trinity Church. Assignment of the Saturday evening service and the Sunday afternoon service varied during Schleiermacher's tenure, depending, in part, upon the presence of an associate pastor, first assigned as a third clergy member of the staff in 1811.[46] The celebration of communion also rotated between services so that the sacrament was offered every Sunday, once a month at each morning service in each tradition. Thus, each month Schleiermacher preached two early morning services, one with and one without communion, and two main services, one with and one without communion.

Access to the worship practices of the various congregations to which Schleiermacher preached prior to his leadership of Trinity Church is indirect due to the absence of sources. As Trillhaas acknowledges, we know very little about the prayers and readings or anything else which might be called a liturgy from published sources.[47] This does not mean, however, that there are no published indications of the structure of ordinary worship. The published sermons themselves provide at least three clues. In an 1831 sermon Schleiermacher referred to the Epistle lesson for the day as making the same point he had just made from the preaching text out of John.[48] This suggests that the scripture reading at least occasionally, if not

46. See Reich, *Schleiermacher als Pfarrer* for full details about the request for and eventual assignment of associate pastors and their responsibilities as they changed during Schleiermacher's tenure.

47. Trillhaas, "Der Berliner Prediger," 11. Schmidt, *Lied-Kirchenmusik-Predigt*, provides considerable manuscript evidence concerning festival services during Schleiermacher's leadership at Trinity Church in Berlin. The festival services have some distinctive characteristics, particularly in the music.

48. SW II/2:282 (John 8:56 27.11.1831 P161). Because this study focuses upon the biblical texts which are the subject of sermons, every citation of a sermon will include the following identifying data in parentheses, enabling the reader to have the most significant characteristics of the sermon in question without referring to the text cited: Johannine text (in the form "John chapter:verse"); date preached (day.month.year); sermon number assigned by Meding ("Pxxx") if published. See Meding for other publication locations. Manuscripts are identified by Schleiermacher Nachlass number (SNx) if in the Akademie der Wissenschaften archive, or by "de Gruyter" and the name of the transcriber if in the de Gruyter archive.

regularly, included more than one text, one of which was designated as the preaching text. The *Todtenfest* sermon from 1823 is published with a lengthy prayer at its conclusion.[49] Finally, many of the published sermons include the numbers of three hymns underneath the title.[50] Thus, the published sermons name four components of worship: preaching, scripture reading or readings, prayer, and hymn singing.

Working from a combination of several pieces of Schleiermacher's correspondence from late in his career and the documents from his public disagreement with the liturgy prescribed for the union church in 1829, Bernhard Schmidt has documented the service Schleiermacher used from 1829 until his death. As you can see below, it contains the components that could be surmised from details attendant to some of the published sermons. There is strong reason to believe that the major components were the same throughout Schleiermacher's preaching career whenever he was serving the congregation to which he was preaching.[51] Schmidt reconstructs the 1829 service as follows:[52]

> *Congregational hymn*—different each service, chosen to go with the preaching theme
>
> *Opening words:*
>
> "Our help is in the name of the Lord, who made heaven and earth."
>
> *Confession:*
>
> "All compassionate God and Father! In deep humility we recognize and acknowledge before you [*Dir*] our manifold sins and offenses. Mercifully look down on us and forgive us who are penitent all our sins, for the sake of your beloved Son, our savior, Jesus Christ.
>
> Lord, have mercy on us and hear us favorably!
>
> *Reformed morning prayer:*
>
> "Gracious and faithful God, thou who has caused to shine upon us the clear light of thy Gospel, by which we may rightly know thee and thy will and learn how we are to live and reach a blessed death, we beseech thee sanctify us by thy Spirit that we may ever the more renounce the world and all worldly desires of the heart and seek our joy in serving you in holiness and righteousness, as is pleasing to you, through Jesus Christ our Lord.

49. SWII/4:364–65 (John 6:39–40 23.11.1823 P74).

50. Songsheets for services during one period at Trinity Church, Berlin are the subject of research by Virmond, "Liederblätter," 275–93.

51. Schmidt, *Lied—Kirchenmusik—Predigt*, 357–58.

52. Ibid., 328–32, my translation.

Almighty God and Father, for whose sake we are all gathered here to celebrate the Lord's Day, open our ears and hearts that we may hear thy holy word and hold to it in purity of heart, confidently call upon thee, and prepare ourselves for blessedness all the remaining days of our short life, that with angelic tongues and hearts we may with all chosen humans and angels honor and praise thee for all eternity. Amen.

Epistle or Gospel reading:

"The Epistle/Gospel stands written:" (reading of the text)

After the reading:

"The God of peace sanctify you [*euch*] utterly and your entire spirit, soul and body be kept blameless until the future of our Lord Jesus Christ. Faithful is the one who calls you [*euch*], the one who will do it."

Sermon hymn—different each service, sung by the congregation or choir

Sermon:

Church prayer (Kirchengebet)—see Appendix B for the traditional Reformed pattern for this lengthy prayer containing general intercessions

Lord's Prayer:

"Our Father, who art in heaven, hallowed . . . Amen.

Blessing:

"The Lord bless you and keep you, the Lord make his face to shine upon you, and be gracious unto you, the Lord lift his countenance upon you and give you peace. Amen."

Short congregational hymn—different each service, related to preaching theme

This order of worship and the specific choices for the opening words, confession, and benediction that were used regularly at Trinity Church late in Schleiermacher's tenure there are consistent with the earlier Reformed liturgy prior to creation of the union church in Prussia and the uniting of the Lutheran and Reformed congregations of Trinity Church in 1820. The prescribed union church liturgy of 1829 offered two prayers that, when read together, were substantially the traditional "Reformed morning prayer." Schleiermacher evidently used them together as a regular practice. He seems to have retained these familiar features of worship piety in order to support the piety of his congregation, even though he provided detailed criticism in *Christian Faith* of the adequacy of some of the language used in the liturgy when that language was used to construct church doctrine.

Published sermons indicate that on many occasions the sermon itself also began with prayer. For example, an 1806 sermon on John 15:9, 14, 15 begins with the following prayer:

> Lord almighty, holy one, thou who dost unfold thine eternal government, ever the same, in divers ways before the eyes of human beings, that, in following thy higher paths, they may delight, first, in the loveliness of thy favor, given the transient harmony of our shortsighted wishes, then, in turn, be startled in face of the unsearchable power that, moving in directions they cannot follow and by utterances they know not how to explain, often threaten to shatter all that they have somehow created or fostered in caring for their own interests or even thinking for the commonweal. Do thou enlighten for us the eyes of the spirit, that everywhere we may recognize thee, ever the same wise Father, ever full of love, and everywhere take within ourselves the domain that thou hast entrusted to thy Son. Do thou strengthen in us a nobler sensibility that we may treat all others in such a way that in us and through us only thy will may be done. Even now, our whole desire is turned to these things. To that end, may this hour of communal devotion be blessed also.[53]

The earlier published sermons on Johannine texts are particularly likely to open with such a prayer.

The final church prayers (*Kirchengebete*) included intercessions for the congregation's sick, women in childbirth, and the mentally ill, as well as for church leadership, the king, and those who serve him.[54] Appendix B provides the text of a version of this prayer that was included in the prescribed union church liturgy of 1829. It was retained from an earlier liturgy from 1713. It is very long, though the accompanying rubrics allow it to be shortened. The content of prayer after the sermon drew Schleiermacher's attention and concern in particular. His reflection about that content reveals his understanding of the relationship between preaching and the prayers:

> . . . many preachers, including myself, find it appropriate, when the sermon leads to a closing prayer through reference of its con-

53. SW II/1:204 (John 15:9, 14, 15 17.8.1806 P16). In August of 1806 Napoleon's army was advancing across German lands and overran Halle defeating the Prussian army in October 1806.

54. *Ueber die neue Liturgie*, 13.

> tent, to combine this prayer with the general intercessions, which constitute the essence of church prayer. . . . and I have always believed that if I have in this connection followed only the order of thoughts of the previously written prayer, and have not overlooked any main point, then the liturgy is experienced in its complete authority.[55]

This suggests that Schleiermacher did not deem it necessary to read prepared prayers any more than prepared sermon texts. It also implies that the connection between the sermon and the prayer that followed was often, perhaps always, close.

There are many published prayers accompanying Schleiermacher's sermons, but very few accompanying sermons on Johannine texts. One exemplar, at the end of an 1832 sermon on John 16:32, carefully reflects the themes of the sermon but does not reflect the themes commonly found in the 1713 *Kirchengebet*.

> Ah yes, all-bountiful God and Father, let not the remembrance of thy Son's suffering on earth be in vain, even in us; by his victory, may we be secured in our faith in thine eternal reign, founded by him; may we dedicate all our powers ever more earnestly, more undividedly, to thy service. In that spirit, we do pray thee, in the name of him who thou hast placed with us for our redemption and righteousness, for our being made wise and being sanctified. Amen.[56]

Since this sermon was not preached at Trinity Church, it is not clear from this rare Johannine exemplar whether the prayer reflects his typical practice.[57]

The central importance of preaching to the worship service is suggested by at least two very different sources. The 1820 tract to members of the two Trinity Church congregations concerning the changes resulting from their movement toward union speaks in detail about a number of aspects of worship practices. Consistently throughout, the occasions for worship are referred to as "early sermon," "main sermon," and "preparation" (*Frühpredigt, Hauptpredigt, Vorbereitung*) rather than as "worship" (*Gottesdienst*).[58] An

55. *Ueber die neue Liturgie*, 8, my translation.

56. SW I/3:238 (John 16:32 1.4.1832 Laetare P172). This sermon was preached in the Parochial Church, not Trinity Church.

57. I refer the reader to Schmidt, *Lied—Kirchenmusik—Predigt*, for more detailed and comprehensive analysis of Schleiermacher's prayers than the sample of sermons on Johannine texts allows.

58. "An die Mitglieder" (author not specified, the tract closes with reference to the three pastors—Schleiermacher, Marheinecke, and Herzberg—and with best wishes from the consistory superintendents).

unappreciative worshipper who came to hear Schleiermacher guest preach in the French Dom in Berlin provides another clue. He complains about "finally" coming to the preaching as if nothing else in the service is of great significance.[59] This service opened with the singing of several hymns, for which the purchase of a songsheet was required. It is not clear whether the extended opening hymn singing was typical of Schleiermacher's own pastorates. Use of songsheets was typical of Trinity Church, but they usually contained only three hymns. What is clear from this report is the importance of the preaching as the central event in the service.

It is also clear from examination of song sheets printed for use in particular services that the selection of hymns and adaptations of the hymn texts contributed to a unified worship experience unfolding the theme of the preaching. Bernhard Schmidt has demonstrated this in his analysis of festival worship materials from Trinity Church in the de Gruyter archive.[60] This practice is consistent with Schleiermacher's emphasis in his Practical Theology lectures on the organic unity of worship[61] and his account of the relationship between aesthetics and worship.[62] The consistency of festival worship with his theoretical account suggests that ordinary worship probably was also designed to be a unified experience through all its elements—liturgy, prayer, hymns, and preaching.

Brief Remarks on Style

From the various representations of Schleiermacher's preaching several consistent stylistic features emerge. Although the physical distance from pulpit to pew or standing place may have been substantial, Schleiermacher's address to the congregation was intimate. In fact, it was so consistent in this regard that the *Sämmtliche Werke*, collected works, abbreviates the most common forms. The congregations were "friends" and "beloved" and were addressed in the familiar rather than formal plural. This address is a prominent aspect of the directness represented in the preaching transcripts.

The style of developing an argument that recurred repeatedly in Schleiermacher's preaching consisted of presenting his interpretation as a clarification of possible misunderstandings of the text. Early in a sermon a potential misreading of the biblical text was identified. This misreading might arise, according to Schleiermacher, because of an apparent conflict

59. Quoted by Urner, "Schleiermacher als Prediger," 17.
60. Schmidt, *Lied-Kirchenmusik-Predigt.*
61. Ibid., 25–38.
62. Ibid., 42–58.

between what Jesus says on different occasions. Or it may be a conflict between what we as readers of the Bible expect and what the text says.[63] Or it may result from there being more than one potentially correct reading, especially of metaphors. (This is also treated as a conflict between readings.)[64] Misreading may also result from a conflict between the Johannine and the Pauline claims about Jesus.[65] Conflicting accounts of events may have been attributed to the perspective of different authors and left in conflict, but conflicting statements from Jesus were unimaginable and required interpretation to reconcile his meaning.[66] The potential for a conflicting reading was taken as the occasion for Schleiermacher to consider the text more fully and to provide a reading of it for the congregation and its faith. The truthfulness of the interpretation he provided was demonstrated by the ability of the interpretation to clarify and resolve the conflict as he initially described it.

Dietrich Seidel pulls many of these features together in a succinct description of Schleiermacher's preaching style:

> Typically, Schleiermacher expresses his thoughts through a rather elaborate, complex sentence structure. In the sermons there is always a developing argument. In the course of one long sentence, then, he often presents a series of ideas so that his audience has to make an extra effort to connect these thoughts with the overall argument. In other words, his preaching style elicits the cooperation of his congregation. The preacher sets out to present consideration of a problem and its solutions. This is done not by simply offering a ready-made solution but by inviting his listeners to use their own imagination and critical faculties for advancing pertinent arguments. As Johannes Bauer has observed, a distinctive characteristic of Schleiermacher's preaching style is that his point of view emerges only gradually from the ideas he offers until it becomes entirely clear, as the result of a search shared by speaker and listener.[67]

Another striking aspect of Schleiermacher's style, from the perspective of early 21st century American preaching, is that he did not use examples or stories from his own (or any contemporary's) experience as illustrations. This does not mean that there is an absence of references to the life of his listeners. Rather, those references are general and inclusive of all present,

63. For an example, see SW II/8:461 (John 6:52–60 12.12.1824 P395).
64. For an example, see SW II/8:457–60 (John 6:52–60 12.12.1824 P395).
65. For an example, see SW II/9:21–22 (John 7:14–24 20.2.1825 P398).
66. For an example, see SW II/8:366–67 (John 5:31–40 11.7.1824 P388).
67. Seidel, "Editor's Introduction," xxiv.

not particular. His illustrations were all from the biblical text. He walked and thought through the text as if the biblical world was familiar rather than strange—almost as though it narrated the lives of his hearers rather than those of a foreign culture and time. The discourses spoken by Jesus to his disciples were understood by Schleiermacher to be directed to all disciples in every time. "As he says that to his disciples, he also says it to us, because they were the totality of those belonging to him. What he says to them he says to the entire Christian church and to the complete community of his own."[68] It is typical of Schleiermacher's preaching to draw direct parallels between events and motivations found in the biblical text and the experience of his listeners.[69] Schleiermacher did not allow the distance commonly experienced in the 21st century between biblical text and us to develop in his preaching.

The source of a preacher's authority functions implicitly in preaching. Although its roots are theological, this voice is also a component of style. Schleiermacher spoke with the voice of the faith he believed he shared with the congregation. He spoke not on his own personal authority but on the authority of the faith that he was confident was visible within him. Thus, he stood on both sides of the Word—hearing the Word with the congregation and also speaking a truth to the congregation that was in some way known to them.

In the lectures on practical theology Schleiermacher made a distinction between sermons and homilies. Both forms of preaching strive for a unity of the parts into a whole, but they are distinguished by the manner through which this unity is achieved. A homily relies upon adherence to the biblical text for its unity. A sermon, in contrast, is unified in a twofold manner through the biblical text and a theme. Although unity is achieved differently, good preaching expresses a unity of thought equally well in either the form of a homily or the form of a sermon.[70] The danger in a sermon form is that although the theme relates to the biblical text, the biblical text may disappear as everything in the sermon relates to the theme. This disappearance of the biblical text is not desirable.[71] The danger in a homily form is that the artistic unification of the pieces of the homily

68. SW II/9:478 (John 15:1–7 2.7.1826 P430).

69. The Johannine sermons belie Richard Crouter's contention that Schleiermacher typically structured his sermons into exegesis and application sections. The parallels indicated above are common in all sections of the Johannine sermons. See Crouter, "Friedrich Schleiermacher," 25.

70. *Praktische Theologie*, 232.

71. Ibid., 232–33.

may get lost if it follows a biblical text that is not itself unified.[72] Yet, both didactic and historical biblical texts may effectively be used as the subjects for homilies.[73] The practical theology lectures do not mention length as a distinguishing feature between sermons and homilies, as we might expect given late twentieth century American use of the terms.

Cursory examination of the transcriptions of preaching for the two services at Trinity Church leads to the categorization of the early morning service preaching as homilies and the main service preaching as sermons. More careful reading makes this distinction a rule of thumb rather than a precise categorization. As the sermons on Johannine texts are published, the introductions to the early morning homilies are usually very short (8–10 lines), and simply remind the hearer of where they are beginning in the Gospel narrative. In the main service sermons the introductions are much longer (1–2 pages), though their format varies from sermon to sermon. The biblical text may come at the beginning, or it may be read after a paragraph or two of introduction and be followed by another paragraph of introduction and the sermon theme. In the sermons for the main service the introduction establishes why the particular text is appropriate for the day or season and concludes either with a statement of the theme for the sermon or with a statement of the main points of the sermon. These sermons tend to be organized around a theme and two main points. The early morning homilies seem to be organized rather as a series of ideas held together by the arrangement of the biblical text.[74]

However, the distinction that Schleiermacher makes in his lectures is less clear in the transcriptions of his own preaching. Some of the main service sermons from very late in Schleiermacher's career are constructed without a tight theme and instead explicitly string together two or three main points.[75] The distinction between homilies and sermons, early morning preaching and main service preaching, is further blurred by the way in which the major points of the main service sermons are attached to the

72. Ibid., 233.

73. Ibid., 767.

74. Trillhaas describes the early morning preaching as more personal than the main service preaching. I do not find this general characterization supported by the sermons on Johannine texts. In fact, I'm not sure I understand what Trillhaas thinks he sees. *Schleiermachers Predigt*, 22.

75. See SW II/4:195–208 (John 1:12–17 5.12.1830 P137) and SW II/3:724–37 (John 1:23–27 22.12.1833 P231). Schleiermacher described his intent in the introductions of both of these transcriptions to provide selected thoughts from biblical texts too rich to mine thoroughly in an hour. There is not a unifying theme, rather the points depend upon the biblical text.

biblical text. These sermons are constructed so that they often appear to the first hearing/reading to follow the logic of the biblical text.

Length of the sermon transcriptions varies. It does not simply correspond to whether the sermon was delivered at the early morning or the main service. Length may correspond to whether or not communion is offered in the service, but records are not sufficiently complete to test this hypothesis. Most of the sermons for which we have a full text take approximately 40 to 50 minutes to read aloud. This is consistent with Schleiermacher's suggestion that a half-hour long sermon is too short, and an hour long sermon is too long.[76] Length of sermons, according to the practical theology lectures, depends upon both the ability of the congregation to listen and whether another service of worship follows.[77]

The earlier discussions of illustration and of the use of the biblical texts in sermons and homilies are two aspects of what it means to describe Schleiermacher as a biblical preacher. Another aspect is his use of biblical texts as the basis for his preaching. Of the 583 published examples of Schleiermacher preaching, all but 13 work with a biblical text. Of these 13, five were preached at a graveside and five were preached at a wedding or anniversary.

The John Sermons and Our Sources for Them

The Gospel of John was Schleiermacher's favorite preaching text. There are three kinds of sources for documenting 228 occasions on which Schleiermacher preached on some portion of John: published sermons, catalogued by Meding;[78] unpublished manuscripts in the Akademie der Wissenschaften Archiv and the Walter de Gruyter Publishing House archive,[79] some of which are outlines and some of which are transcriptions; and notations in Schleiermacher's daily diaries deciphered by Dr. Wolfgang Virmond of the Schleiermacherforschungstelle in Berlin.[80] Until the index of manuscripts in the de Gruyter archive and daily diary citations are pub-

76. *Praktische Theologie*, 214.

77. Ibid.

78. Meding, *Bibliographie*. See also Tice, *Schleiermacher's Sermons*.

79. The de Gruyter Publishing House archive has a collection of some 700 manuscript items which had not been catalogued until 1996. I have not had access to this catalogue-in-process and have worked with only a handful of items from this archive. The Schleiermacher Forschungstelle in Kiel has supervised the cataloguing of this material along with the rest of the known sermons.

80. I am deeply indebted to Wolfgang Virmond for his generous assistance in making his working research on the diaries available to me, and for patiently reading Schleiermacher's handwriting with me.

lished, it is possible to compare the frequency with which Schleiermacher selected Johannine texts to his selection of other texts only by examining the published sermons. Twenty-two percent of all his published sermons use Johannine texts. Limiting the comparison to his preference just among Gospel texts, forty-one percent of the published sermons on a Gospel text use John. Sermons on John span Schleiermacher's career from as early as 1791 to as late as New Year's 1834, just weeks before his death. Although there are Johannine texts to which Schleiermacher returns repeatedly throughout his career, no single pericope dominates his preaching on the Gospel of John.

Published sermons document 129 of the 228 preaching events on Johannine texts. Most of these are transcriptions providing a full sermon text. In only rare cases does a manuscript for one of these transcriptions still exist, and often this manuscript is clearly not the source used for publication. The sermons published by Zimmer and by Bauer are outlines.[81] Manuscripts in Schleiermacher's hand are available for many of these outlines. Comparison of some of them shows that Zimmer did not always include the complete manuscript in his publication of individual outlines.[82] The 99 unpublished preaching events are documented by 14 manuscript outlines of sermons, 18 manuscript transcriptions of sermons, and 67 notations in the daily diaries. A complete listing of the sermons and their sources is found in Appendix A.

In addition to this categorization of Johannine sermons by sources, it is also useful to distinguish those sermons preached as part of a sermon series begun on April 13, 1823, and concluded on May 20, 1827. In 95 sermons Schleiermacher preached seriatim through the entire Gospel of John.[83] For most of the series, the sermons were preached at the early morning service, but beginning in Lent 1827 (March 4, 1827) every sermon we have record of Schleiermacher having preached (early morning, main service, and the special days: Good Friday, Easter Monday) followed

81. Zimmer, "erster Amtsthätigkeit," 281–90, 369–78, and Zimmer, *aus 1800*; Bauer, *Ungedruckte Predigten*, and Bauer, *Patriotischer Prediger.*

82. Appendix A notes both manuscript and publication data and notes those instances in which I have had opportunity to compare the two and have discovered omissions in the published work.

83. In January 1822 Schleiermacher began to select his sermon texts for the early Sunday morning service by moving seriatim through Philippians. The success of this 29 sermon series led him immediately upon its conclusion to begin a series on the Gospel of John. Other much shorter series on Pauline texts followed. The only other series on a Gospel was a series on Mark, begun in August 1831 and ending with his death in 1834 without completing the book. This latter series comprises 87% of his preaching on Mark.

the progression of the Johannine text until treatment of the Gospel was completed on the fifth Sunday in Eastertide (May 20, 1827).

The first 74 sermons in the John series were published in the *Sämmtliche Werke* II/8 and II/9 after Schleiermacher's death. Transcriptions of eight additional sermons on John 17:1–13 and 18:1–38 are as yet unpublished. The dates and biblical texts for two sermons on 17:14–24 and the final eleven sermons on 18:38—21:25 are found in the daily diary for 1827.[84]

The series addresses every verse of John with two exceptions. John 8:1–11 is omitted entirely.[85] The critical edition of the Greek Testament published in 1796 by Griesbach and found in Schleiermacher's library at his death brackets this text in John.[86] Perhaps Schleiermacher determined that the status of the pericope as a later addition to John was reason to omit it. He does not mention the omission in the sermons on texts preceding and following. Nor is there record of his preaching on the text at any other point in his career.[87] He does, however, address the text in his notes to himself on the Gospel.[88]

The second omission in the series is of John 6:26. This verse is found without critical comment in Griesbach. Unlike the omission of 8:1–11, the historicity of 6:26 is not at issue. The omission is probably a transcription or publishing error, because the content of 6:26 is touched upon in

84. See Appendix A for details about these sermons. I have been told by the Schleiermacher Forschungstelle in Kiel that transcriptions for the 21 unpublished sermons in the series were found in the de Gruyter archive. Schmidt analyzes one of these unpublished transcripts in *Lied-Kirchenmusik-Predigt*, 419–23.

85. This is the story of the woman caught in adultery.

86. Griesbach, *Novum Testamentum Graece* (1796). This critical edition of the Greek Testament is only one of many editions of the Greek Testament in Schleiermacher's library, according to the listing provided by Meckenstock. I have cited it because it appears to be the most widely used critical edition, reappearing in several editions and reprintings. Unfortunately we do not know which volumes in his library Schleiermacher relied upon most often. For the listing of Schleiermacher's library at the time of his death see Meckenstock, *Schleiermachers Bibliothek*.

87. The record of Schleiermacher's preaching is pieced together from sources that leave significant gaps in our knowledge. One cannot argue that Schleiermacher "never" preached on any particular topic or text; we may only note that it is not recorded. A conservative estimate of the total of Schleiermacher's preaching is 50 times a year for 40 years, that is 2,000 sermons. We have record of no more than about 1,000 of these, of which 583 are published. See Meding, *Bibliographie*, for data on the published sermons. Data from the diaries and a complete list of unpublished manuscripts await publication.

88. SN 8 "Zum Johannes Evangelium" (Akademie der Wissenschaften, Berlin), 71–72. This manuscript in the Akademie der Wissenschaften archive contains Schleiermacher's notes on John arranged verse by verse and covering the entire Gospel. It is not dated. I have not used it extensively in this study because the manuscript contains innumerable abbreviations in poor handwriting and consequently is extremely difficult to read accurately.

the sermon on 6:16–25.[89] The only intentional omission from the series appears to be John 8:1–11.

The group of seven sermons on biblical texts from John 1:35–51 form one of the larger concentrations of Schleiermacher's preaching on Johannine texts. Their characteristics facilitate discussion of the typical features and problems the corpus of Johannine sermons present to interpreters. John 1:35–51 narrates the call of the first disciples of Jesus, with particular emphasis upon the role that a person who believes in Jesus plays in helping other persons come to a faith response of their own. Following the progression of verse numbers,[90] these sermons are as follows:

A. John 1:35–44 (1810) published, enlarged outline

B. John 1:35–51 (5.1.1812) published transcription and published outline

C. John 1:45ff (20.12.1795) published outline and manuscript outline

D. John 1:46 (9.12.1827) 3-line outline from the daily diary

E. John 1:47–51 (15.1.1832) published transcription main service[91]

F. John 1:35–42 (13.7.1823) published transcription, part of series in early morning service

G. John 1:43–51 (27.7.1823) published transcription, part of series in early morning service

Unpublished sermons may be sermon outlines in Schleiermacher's own hand or transcriptions written by persons who were in the congregation. Most of the early sermon outlines were collected in notebooks by Schleiermacher, probably well after they were preached.[92] That is the case for the outline C. The manuscript SN 51 (containing C), identified as sermons in Landsberg, begins with sermons from 1802 and then proceeds to sermons from 1795 and 1796, making it clear that the earlier sermons were copied into the manuscript. What improvements or omissions occurred in the outlines between the preaching of them and the recording of them are dif-

89. SW II/8:402–15 (John 6:16–25 17.10.1824 P391).

90. Because the focus of this study is upon how Schleiermacher interprets this Gospel, it is more illuminating to list the sermons by the biblical text rather than by the date preached.

91. Designating this sermon as a main service sermon is an informed guess. The sermons the week previous and the week following are both in the Mark series, an early morning service series. If the normal practice was followed, then the intervening week would have been a main service sermon. This is further suggested by the use of a non-Marcan text.

92. Some of the individual outlines from these notebooks have been published by Zimmer and Bauer, but none of the notebooks has been published in a form that replicates the manuscript.

ficult to identify. If Schleiermacher were intending to record outlines for possible reuse, it is likely that he recorded the improvements that occurred to him as a result of preaching and consequent reflection upon its effect. Thus, even for the sources from Schleiermacher's own hand, the text or outline of the sermon has a life independent of the preaching itself.

Item D is an anomaly, which further illustrates the distance between preaching and the record of it. This item consists of three lines recorded in Schleiermacher's diary, the outline of his sermon that day. These lines provide only a general idea of the two main parts of the sermon; alone they provide no clues to its development. This is the only instance among the John sermons of the diaries providing an outline of a sermon.

The distance between preaching event and sermon text is even wider in the texts that are transcriptions, in part because they involve a second person listening, remembering, and recording. Dawn DeVries suggests that the transcriptions provide a better sense than sermons Schleiermacher himself transcribed or corrected as to how he sounded in the pulpit.[93] However, comparison of two different transcriptions for the same sermon make very evident the strong influence of the person transcribing the sermon on the result. The choice of wording, extent of development of points, and sometimes the content of development is significantly different between the published transcriptions on John 14:7—16:15 and the handwritten transcriptions in Sethe 1826b.[94] Even if this is only an indication of the lesser abilities of one or another transcriber, it reminds those of us who intend to interpret Schleiermacher's preaching that we are working with a textual account filtered through memory, rather than having direct access to the preaching itself.

Sermons published by Schleiermacher late in his life, such as item E, usually were transcriptions, which Schleiermacher then corrected and improved, and may have enlarged for reading.[95] We may assume that these sermon texts express the content of Schleiermacher's thought, but as a result of enlargements and improvements they are not word-for-word transcriptions of how Schleiermacher expressed himself in the pulpit. This distinction is important precisely because of Schleiermacher's understanding of preaching. It is not only the verbal content of the sermon, it is the total

93. Dawn DeVries, "Introduction" in *Servant of the Word*, 5.

94. See Appendix A for a complete listing of the sermons on John 14:7—16:15 in the sermon series.

95. Enlargement is suggested as a possibility by Schleiermacher's comments in the introduction to the first collection of sermons he published. Since one can read faster than one can preach, a published sermon may be somewhat longer than its spoken presentation (SW II/1:7).

impression of the preacher and his or her faith as expressed in the pulpit which makes preaching efficacious. Schleiermacher intended to communicate more than the verbal content of his sermons when he preached. My point here is that these transcriptions cannot be assumed to be complete accounts of preaching events.

Many of the transcriptions were published after Schleiermacher's death and were not corrected by him. Items A, F, and G and the entire published John series from 1823–26 are among these texts. The editor of the first volume of sermons in the John series (SW II/8) claims that these texts are word-for-word transcriptions.[96] We have no way to verify this assertion, nor did he. The existence of manuscript transcriptions for some of the published sermons in the series, and the significant differences between the two transcriptions of the same sermon suggests how unlikely it is that any transcription is an exact verbatim account of the original preaching event.

Some of the sermon outlines from Schleiermacher's early preaching were also published after his death. The faithfulness of the published text to the manuscripts varies greatly. Several of the texts published by Zimmer omit entire sections of the outline found in the handwritten manuscripts.[97] The outlines published by Bauer for which we have original manuscripts agree with those manuscripts and suggest that his transcriptions are reliable.

Item B allows us to consider the relationship between these outlines and their full development into a sermon. The outline was published by Bauer in 1908, and a transcription was published by Schleiermacher himself in 1814, at least two years after the sermon was delivered.[98] The outline identifies points without reference to the thematic biblical text for the sermon, but the sermon transcription clothes these concepts completely in the biblical narrative. This narrative style emphasizes some aspects of the logical structure of the outline over others. For example, a contrast is developed within each point of the outline between Jesus as the model and emulation of him; but the narrative style of the text focuses upon Jesus, and emulation is often relegated to a single closing sentence in the paragraph. This weighting of one point more than the other is not at all evident in the outline. Thus, interpreters must be especially cautious in

96. SW II/8: vii.

97. I have not been able to compare and correct all of Zimmer's publication of sermons on John with the available manuscripts. However, Appendix A notes the published texts, which I know are incomplete from comparison with some of the manuscripts available in Berlin.

98. Bauer, *Patriotischer Prediger*, 355–56; SW II/1:387–99.

making judgments about Schleiermacher's early preaching based upon these outlines alone. They are logical structures and give little indication of how sermons are finally developed.

This review of the kinds of sources that represent Schleiermacher's preaching leads us to caution in how closely we identify the transcriptions and outlines with the nuances and fullness of the preaching events themselves. There is some interplay between transcribers' abilities and events that influenced their memories, also between subsequent events and contexts that influence the perspective of each historian. The most accurate characterization of Schleiermacher's preaching identifies those features that seem to be consistent across the many different types of representations. Rather than particular interpretations of pericopes, or recurring points of doctrine, or even favorite texts that remain favorite for long periods of time, what remains consistent in the representations of Schleiermacher's preaching on John are the presuppositions that lie behind the preaching. Chapter three will support this contention in detail.

Development in Schleiermacher's Preaching

In his large work on Schleiermacher's sermons, Wolfgang Trillhaas treats the theory of Schleiermacher's preaching as if the preaching remains the same throughout Schleiermacher's career.[99] Trillhaas derives the theory primarily from the 1850 publication of the practical theology lectures, a publication developed by editing various student notebooks and notes in Schleiermacher's hand from several different years, but organized around the notes for the 1830/31 lectures. Thus the theory is derived from a source that comes late in Schleiermacher's career. In spite of his treatment of the theory as consistent, Trillhaas also notes changes in Schleiermacher's preaching. He describes the first collection of sermons, published in 1801, as being scholarly addresses rather like the *Speeches*.[100] He then notes a change occurring about 1810, a change in color and content, which continued to the end of Schleiermacher's life.[101] Pinpointing one precise change in the years around 1810 is practically impossible, because so few representations of Schleiermacher's preaching from the years prior and succeeding have been preserved.[102] Other scholars have avoided the question

99. Trillhaas, *Schleiermachers Predigt.*

100. Ibid., 23.

101. Trillhaas, *Schleiermachers Predigt*, 26.

102. The listing of published sermons by Meding, *Bibliographie* shows the following: 1807—5; 1808—2; 1809—2; 1810—27; 1811—none; 1812—14; 1813—2; 1814—none; 1815—1; 1816—none.

of changes by focusing upon preaching prior to Schleiermacher's tenure at Trinity Church.[103] A more illuminating result emerges when we examine how Schleiermacher interpreted the same biblical text at various times in his career.

There is significant variation in the themes which Schleiermacher developed in the six sermons on John 1:35–51 between 1795 and 1832. Tracing the changes in how Schleiermacher preached upon this text provides a way to note changes in his preaching across his career. The outlines of a development appear to be present.

In the 1795 sermon (Landsberg),[104] the themes distance the listener from the disciples. The biblical text becomes the occasion for thinking about first impressions and how unreliable they are and also about how unreliable prejudices either for or against persons are on the basis of external relationships. Finally, miracles are unreliable and therefore we should have a better foundation for our faith than Nathanael had for his. This seems to be as much a sermon on friendship as it is on Christian faith, particularly since it is not clear from the outline why the third point is connected to the first two points.

The 1810 sermon (Trinity Church),[105] an expanded outline, still distances us from the text: "what we learn from the Redeemer's choice of disciples." However, the points addressed in the outline have to do with the life of the church: The disciples are and remain a diverse group of personalities; all are equal in importance regardless of how well known they are; beginnings of extraordinary relationships are often unremarkable. In this sermon outline, faith and faithfulness are reiterated in the conclusion, as they are in all of the four later sermons.

The decisive change in emphasis appears in the sermon transcription from 5.1.1812 (Trinity Church).[106] Here we are explicitly asked to imitate the pattern of relationship and its beginnings that are traced in the sermon's reading of the biblical text. The relationships that are considered are all relationships between individuals and Jesus. This sermon is the most clearly organized of this entire group of sermons.

The 1823 sermon transcriptions (Trinity Church),[107] which were early morning sermons, are less centrally organized around one theme.

103. Seifert, *Die Theologie des jungen Schleiermachers*; Jung, *Der Erlösungsbegriff*; Meier-Dörkin, *Die Theologie der frühen Predigten*.

104. SN 51 (Akademie der Wissenschaftenen, Berlin), 89–90 and Bauer, *Patriotischer Prediger*, 353–54 (John 1:45ff 20.12.1795 P565).

105. SW II/7:575–79 (John 1:35–44 1810 Season of Epiphany P360).

106. SW II/1:387–99 (John 1:35–51 5.1.1812 P33).

107. SW II/8:85–99 (John 1:35–42 13.7.1823 P368) and SW II/8, 100–111 (John

They explore the relationships between the Redeemer and the disciples, particularly how these relationships began, while reiterating that it is the relationship to the Redeemer rather than the content of teaching or the manner in which one is called that is most important. We are not simply learning from the biblical text; the sermon takes us into its relational matrix. It is no longer a matter of imitation.

The 1832 sermon transcription (Trinity Church)[108] considers how the relationship between the Redeemer and the various disciples is secured. This reflection leads to a consideration of the various preconditions for faith in the Redeemer and for identifying the importance of continuing to grow in faith after an initial relationship is established. In these last three sermons Schleiermacher identified his listeners as being in continuity with the first disciples; what we learn from the disciples applies directly to ourselves because their story is our story.

Two closely related lines of development are evident. The first has to do with the relationship Schleiermacher drew between his audience and the biblical text. Initially the text was an object for objective consideration. Eventually the text and the listener's own experience were fused, so that the text interprets the listener as much as the listener interprets the text. This change was gradual from the early to the very mature preaching. It cannot be located in one portion of Schleiermacher's preaching career. The second line of development began with attention to human relationships and becomes focused specifically upon one relationship, the relationship of persons of faith to the Redeemer, which is the matrix for faith.

Describing all of the various threads of development that might be traced through the sermons is beyond the scope of this work.[109] However, the presence of developments during his preaching career is yet another factor complicating any effort to characterize Schleiermacher's preaching as a whole.

Conclusion

The variety of circumstances under which Schleiermacher preached, the number of factors that influence our sources of sermon texts, and the developments in his preaching during his forty-year career as a preacher all make the sermons a resource to be used with wisdom. As proof-texts for particular points of dogma, individual sermons are tentative

1:43–51 27.7.1823 P369).

108. SW II/3:156–68 (John 1:47–51 15.1.1832 P166).

109. Other developmental threads include Schleiermacher's understanding of the Holy Spirit.

evidence. In contrast, the larger picture across a body of the sermons may be more reliably drawn using the variety of textual sources, either examining a particular period in Schleiermacher's life, or investigating his interpretation of a biblical text across his lifetime.

I suggest an analogy as the basis for one effective model for working with the sermons. Our sources for Schleiermacher preaching provide us with representations of that preaching that have affinities to impressionist paintings. The closer we attempt to examine details in isolation from the whole, the less those details reveal. But the overall impression is rich and evocative and invites attention to particular interests: in the case of impressionist painting to light and color, in the case of Schleiermacher's preaching to the presuppositions with which he began when he preached. Schleiermacher's preaching on the Gospel of John discloses three such presuppositions. The delineation of these presuppositions is the subject of the next chapter.

3

Schleiermacher's Interpretive Frame for Preaching on John: Three Presuppositions

In his preaching Schleiermacher invited his first hearers and his later readers (including ourselves) to think together about the Gospel text in order to sharpen our perception of the Redeemer and deepen our relationship to him and, through him, to God. When the reader accepts this invitation from Schleiermacher and pays particular attention to both his selection of texts and his interpretation of them, a set of three presuppositions that demarcate his interpretive approach to Jesus emerge. With these presuppositions providing his interpretive frame of reference, Schleiermacher developed a coherent and vivid picture of the Redeemer in his preaching.

This chapter builds the case for the presence of these presuppositions by examining Schleiermacher's preaching on the Johannine pericopes that were most significant in his career of preaching on John. Following a brief summary of Schleiermacher's critical attitude toward the Johannine text, as expressed in his preaching on John, this chapter discusses groups of sermons on particular pericopes, following the order of the Johannine text. This arrangement facilitates attention to consistencies and inconsistencies in interpretation across Schleiermacher's career. The chapter closes by gathering together the evidence for each of the presuppositions and sketching the outlines of the picture of the Redeemer formed through Schleiermacher's preaching on John.

The following three presuppositions will emerge in the course of analyzing the sermons: 1) It is apparent to all who come into the sphere of Jesus' influence that he is the Redeemer; 2) Redemption is available through the Redeemer prior to his death and resurrection; 3) Redemption is directly associated with incorporation into a community of Christians. What these presuppositions mean and how they function in Schleiermacher's interpretation of and preaching on John will become clear as the chapter progresses.

Schleiermacher's Critical Attitude toward the Text Expressed in His Preaching on John

Schleiermacher consistently preached on the Johannine text as though the text is an accurate eyewitness account by someone who had close familiarity with and faith in Christ. This position is clearest in the sermon series begun in 1823, only three years after Bretschneider published his challenge to scholarly acceptance of John as an eyewitness to the life of Jesus.[1] The introductory remarks to the first sermon inaugurating the four-year long John series state what was usually assumed in the sermons: John was uniquely able to comprehend and therefore to record the deep speech of Jesus. Schleiermacher did not provide argumentation for the truthfulness of this position in the sermons, but he stated the position clearly and forcefully. He said that what was expressed in the written word of the Gospel of John is the fullness of divinity (*Gottheit*) that dwelt in the Redeemer and that spoke through him.[2] This evaluation of John did not preclude the historical accuracy of the synoptic Gospels,[3] but what distinguished the Gospel of John, in Schleiermacher's view, was that John narrated events, including miracles,[4] only when they were necessary to understand what the Redeemer said.[5] It was what was said which was crucial in Schleiermacher's preached interpretation of the Gospel of John. And he preached John as a trustworthy witness and scribe of what was said. One of his longer comments on this point occurred in 1825: John did not mix his own opinion or judgment into his account, not even to fill in and make the invisible

1. Bretschneider, *Probabilia*. In the furious debate following publication of this work, Bretschneider retracted his position.

2. SW II/8:3–4. Schleiermacher did not read the Gospel of John as an exhaustive expression of the speech of the Redeemer. He did, however, believe that John recorded everything essential for faith, and referred to John 20:30–31 for support of both points.

3. For instance, SW II/8:55–67 (John 1:24–28 15.6.1823 P366) plays John 1 off against Matthew 3:11 in order to provide an account that makes both versions historically credible. For all citations of sermons, material in parentheses is the biblical text (chapter: verse), the date preached (day.month.year), and if published the sermon number provided by Meding in *Bibliographie*.

4. In the Gospel of John many of the miracles are designated as "signs," and seven of these are specifically counted.

5. SW II/9:322–23 (John 12:20–26 5.2.1826 P419) and SW II/8:332 (John 5:16–23 13.6.1824 P386).

cohesion between events and the words of the Lord explicit. John was a genuinely accurate witness and desired to do nothing other than what he did: that is, to convey what he himself had seen and heard. This desire itself is the strongest sign and the greatest perfection of an accurate witness. John conveyed what the Lord himself said and what resulted further from it.[6] The Gospel of John was written accurately by an eyewitness, and through it we have direct access to the words of Jesus.

Schleiermacher was inconsistent in his acknowledgment of the role of editorial judgment in the content of the Johannine text. The lack of record in John 1 of what Jesus said to Philip and the others when they first met Jesus and spent the day with him was interpreted by Schleiermacher as an editorial silence. Schleiermacher assumed that John, who he believed was the author of the account, was the second, unnamed disciple who followed Jesus when John the Baptist pointed Jesus out to the disciples (John 1:15–17). Thus, John knew that a good deal was said on that day, because he was present. Yet, the Gospel does not record it. Schleiermacher explained that this was because John knew that what was said later was more important and encompassed what was said on that first day, so John did not include the discourse from the first day. The silence was editorial, in Schleiermacher's judgment. Yet, his interpretation of the next pericope (Nathanael meets Jesus) was unquestioning of the text's veracity in reporting events as if no editorial decision-making might have been involved in the Johannine account. Schleiermacher's explanation of the enigmatic answer Jesus gave to Nathanael's question ("How do you know me?") was that the others present were not supposed to understand the answer. Further, Nathanael's disproportionate response of faith showed that he understood a communication clearly directed toward him alone.[7] Thus, in Schleiermacher's reading of this text, the obscurity resided not in the textual account but in the original event.

This kind of variation in his critical stance toward the text clearly indicates that other principles of interpretation were operating as Schleiermacher preached. It is not fair to say that Schleiermacher took no account of principles of textual criticism,[8] but other presuppositions did take precedence in his preached interpretation of John. We turn now to examine

6. SW II/9:283 (John 11:41–54 18.12.1825 P416).

7. SW II/8:100–111 (John 1:43–51 27.7.1823 P369).

8. Note, for instance, his omission of John 8:1–11 from his preaching on John, an omission most likely made on text critical grounds. See chapter two for discussion of this omission.

how those presuppositions influenced his preaching on specific Johannine texts.

Pericopes from John

In the Beginning Was the Logos: John 1:1–18

Schleiermacher did not generally adopt the terminology of Logos Christology in his preaching on John. The only record of his preaching on the opening verses of John 1 is the sermon that began his seriatim preaching through the Gospel in 1823.[9] This sermon did use the Logos terminology of the biblical text, interpreting it through the later verse John 1:14 ("the Word/Logos became flesh and dwelt among us"), and it is atypical at precisely this point. Schleiermacher did not reject Logos terminology when it was presented by the text, but neither did he introduce it into his preaching when it did not appear in his preaching text. Much more typical was wording like the following, taken from a sermon on John 1:12–17 in which Logos terminology is present in the biblical text and could just as easily have been used by Schleiermacher:

> . . . those who look to the only-begotten Son find eternal life in him, because his glory was fullness of grace and truth. Whoever looked to him with desire for help and with unbiased eyes must also have sensed the spiritual power that dwelt in him, as it began to work upon them; . . .[10]

In this sermon, as in that of 1812, Schleiermacher alluded to the portion of John 1:14 in which the Son is said to reflect the glory of the Father. Who Jesus is in himself, the Logos, is less important in Schleiermacher's use of the text than what Jesus does, dwelling among us as the only-begotten Son, revealing the Father's glory.[11]

In his second *Letter to Dr. Lücke,* published in 1829 as a response to criticisms of his dogmatic work *Christian Faith*, Schleiermacher said: "I would have wished to construct the work so that at every point the reader would be made aware that the verse John 1:14 is the basic text for all dogmatics, just as it should be for the conduct of ministry as a whole."[12] This priority did not translate into frequent preaching on the text.[13] As will be

9. SW II/8:3–14 (John 1:1–5 13.4.1823 P362).

10. SW II/4:205 (John 1:12–17 5.12.1830 P137). Unless otherwise noted, all translations of sermons are my own.

11. SW II/1:387–99 (John 1:35–51 5.1.1812 P33).

12. Duke and Fiorenza, trans., *Letters to Lücke,* 59.

13. Schleiermacher is recorded to have used John 1:14 as preaching text on four oc-

shown, Schleiermacher frequently referred to John 6:68 ("Lord, to whom shall we go? You have the words of eternal life") and John 12:24 ("Unless a grain of wheat dies it does not bear fruit"), incorporating paraphrases of one or the other of these texts into his preaching on other Johannine texts. In contrast, Schleiermacher tended not to paraphrase the first phrase of John 1:14 and use it in his preaching: "And the Word became flesh and dwelt among us." When he did refer to the verse, it was the second half that was used: "we have learned to know his glory, glory of the only Son of the Father." The Redeemer, the name Schleiermacher came to use almost exclusively for Jesus Christ in his later preaching, emphasizes who Jesus is to us. The Logos invites speculation about inner Trinitarian relations. The conception of the Redeemer as incarnate presence of the Father is expressed in Schleiermacher's preaching on Johannine texts, but he avoided Logos terminology.

The Call of the Disciples

Schleiermacher interpreted the Johannine description of the call of the disciples as paradigmatic for how persons come to faith. He preached upon some portion of John 1:35–51 in all three phases of his preaching career.[14] In the earliest extant sermon on this text, Schleiermacher said that we can do better than the way Nathanael came to the Redeemer.[15] Because Nathanael was a negative example in Schleiermacher's description, a different way of faith was implied. This way was described negatively; it does not rely upon external relationships or circumstances, nor upon miracles, nor upon first impressions. What remains positively is not explicit in the outline of the sermon, and perhaps it was not explicit in the preaching itself. This positive space is roughly the shape of the presupposition that within the sphere of Jesus' influence one knows directly who Jesus is in himself, and it is that encounter which appropriately initiates and motivates faith.

The 1810 sermon read the biblical text from the perspective of the Redeemer selecting his disciples (rather than from the perspective of those

casions (1814, 1823, 1829, 1830), all of them at Trinity Church and three of the four between the publication of the two editions of *Christian Faith*—the same time period in which the *Letters to Lücke* were written. The 1823 sermon was the John series sermon on the text.

14. Generally, I will refer to the preaching through 1806 as "early," and the preaching following the first publication of *Christian Faith* in 1821 as "mature."

15. SN 51 (Akademie der Wissenschaften, Berlin), 89–90 and Bauer, *Patriotischer Prediger,* 353–54 (John 1:45ff 20.12.1795 P565).

choosing to follow).[16] Although the text of the sermon is a cross between an outline and a transcription, and consequently is sketchy in the development of illustration, it appears that Schleiermacher narrated the call of the disciples in such a way that their decisions to follow after encountering Jesus are expected. Someone in the sphere of the Redeemer's influence will decide to follow him as a free decision. The sermon affirmed that the Redeemer received different kinds of people and assumed that those who are received will respond. Schleiermacher did not specify in this sermon how the disciples understood the identity of the one whom they followed. He simply used the name Redeemer, as if he regarded consciousness of Jesus as Redeemer to be a part of the disciples' experience of responding to him.

In a sermon from January 1812 the plausibility of this presupposition was elaborated.[17] "What certainly must have come then, however, and what those men must soon have held regarding Jesus, was trust in the impression that his entire being made upon them."[18] Schleiermacher went on to clarify that this impression was not formed instantly: ". . . they remained with him that entire day and there learned to know his glory as the glory of the only Son of the Father, full of grace and truth, and could confidently say to their friends and brothers: we have found the Messiah."[19] To have spent a day with Jesus was sufficient to come into his sphere of influence. Schleiermacher did not elaborate on how those who spent the day with Jesus would have learned to know his glory. It happened then and Schleiermacher took for granted that it still happens. The elaboration of the presupposition was not complete; it merely showed that the disciples-to-be spent sufficient time with Jesus to come fully into his sphere of influence.

The sermons on John 1:35–51 in 1823 (part of the series on John) laid special emphasis upon the role that preaching has in the evocation of faith. Schleiermacher referred often to Rom 10:17 in these sermons and others.[20] The various threads Schleiermacher drew together are evident in part of the 1823 sermon on John 1:43–51:

16. SW II/7:575–79 (John 1:35–44 1810 Season of Epiphany P360).

17. SW II/1:387–99 and Bauer, *Patriotischer Prediger*, 355–56 (John 1:35–51 5.1.1812 P33).

18. SW II/1:395.

19. SW II/1:396.

20. The German text for Rom 10:17 reads: "So kommt der Glaube aus der Predigt, das Predigen aber durch das Wort Christi." This is somewhat different from both the Greek text and the English translation, which do not refer specifically to preaching, but more generally to "that which is heard."

> Faith can have no foundation upon which it may rest with strength other than experience. Faith comes in this respect only from preaching (Rom 10:17)—for the word of Philip was indeed also a sermon—since preaching intends to point out its true object to the attention and hope of a heart that feels its possibility. Preaching, however, gives rise to nothing by itself; rather, the Lord himself must give the power, and now that is also none other than what gives rise to faith, as the entire picture of the life of our Lord, as it stands before us in the holy scriptures and in everything that he, through his Spirit, has already caused to burst forth in the hearts of those who are surely inspired and seized by this faith.[21]

Preaching is important because it provides the listener with direct experience of living faith. Preaching clarifies and directs the emotions to their true purpose, an object that is not foreign but is rather one that the heart recognizes is possible. Preaching itself, however, is only a means to convey the life of the Lord. It is this life that is the power that evokes faith. Those who live in this faith are further inspired by his Spirit. This emphasis on preaching's role in the development of faith was evident much earlier in Schleiermacher's preaching on this text. In 1812 he argued: "Faith comes through preaching, that is the natural way, and so it was natural that the first faith in Jesus came out of the preaching of John [the Baptist]."[22] Because faith comes through preaching, in addition to the preaching of others concerning him, the Son of God himself must also have preached and taught in order to evoke faith. He preached concerning himself.[23]

The two sermons from 1823 and one from 1832 on this biblical text operated within the full presupposition.[24] These three sermons discussed the readiness of Philip and Nathanael to be influenced by Jesus and the role of one person in bringing another into the community where Jesus is experienced. The precise content of this experience was not specified. Schleiermacher thought that Jesus said something to Nathanael that evoked Nathanael's exclamation of faith, but what was said was not paradigmatic. It was the encounter that was paradigmatic. The person of Jesus was efficacious. Consequently, faith may be expressed in many ways, because the person encountered (Jesus) is the same.[25] Across the 37 years' span of preaching on John 1:35–51, Schleiermacher's presupposition that

21. SW II/8:106 (John 1:43–51 27.7.1823 P369).

22. SW II/1:391–2 (John 1:35–51 5.1.1812 P33).

23. SW II/8:92 (John 1:35–42 13.7.1823 P368).

24. SW II/8:85–99 (John 1:35–42 13.7.1823 P368); SW II/8:100–111 (John 1:43–51 27.7.1823 P369); SW II/3:156–68 (John 1:47–51 15.1.1832 P166).

25. SW II/8:85–99 (John 1:35–42 13.7.1823 P368).

those who come into the sphere of Jesus' influence all perceive that he is the Redeemer is evident as the basis for his reading of the biblical text.

The Wedding at Cana

The first of the miracles that the Johannine text names "signs" occurs in John 2—the water turned to wine at Cana.[26] This is a good place to discuss Schleiermacher's interpretation of miracles in the entire Gospel, because he is consistent in his reading of all of them. Generally, Schleiermacher did not choose the signs narratives as preaching texts. Perhaps part of his preference for John is the relatively large proportion of discourse material and smaller number of miracle stories. Yet, he does address the miracles in his seriatim preaching in the John series. Since these are sermons from his mature period, it is not at all surprising that his treatment of the miracles is consistent.

In his series preaching on John 2, Schleiermacher stated the basic position repeated throughout the series: The miracles did not and could not evoke full faith in the Redeemer. This is because the Redeemer is unique and the performance of miracles is *not* unique. The miracles reveal the glory of a prophet, because the prophets also performed miracles. They do not reveal the divinity of Jesus' nature.[27] The divinity of Jesus is revealed in the immediate impression he gives, especially through his words. While preaching on the wedding story, Schleiermacher observed that it was one of the many occasions on which the Redeemer was asked for a sign in order that people might believe. A sign was never provided for this purpose. Schleiermacher concluded that signs occur as a response to faith and love and do not function to elicit faith.[28]

This explanation reappeared the next year when Schleiermacher preached on the miracle in John 5. Jesus was qualitatively different from the prophets and so the testimony to him must also have been different. If the performance of miracles were Jesus' purpose, then his goal would have been complete with the miracles. "And we don't believe that," Schleiermacher stated categorically and without further argument.[29] The reason was suggested in a later sermon that year: ". . . what belongs to the per-

26. The sevens signs in John are: the wedding in Cana (2:1–11), the healing of the official's daughter (4:43–54), the healing at the pool of Bethesda (5:1–15), the feeding of the 5,000 (6:1–15), walking on water (6:16–21), healing the man born blind (9:1–34), and the raising of Lazarus (11:1–44).

27. SW II/8:124 (John 2:1–11 19.10.1823 P370).

28. SW II/8:143–144 (John 2:18–25 16.11.1823 P372).

29. SW II/8:372 (John 5:31–40 11.7.1824 P388).

ishable cannot in and of itself bring forth everlasting life."[30] The goal of the Redeemer's work is bringing forth everlasting life. Healing is perishable, and therefore the miracles could not have been a primary part of the Redeemer's purpose. Pieces of this train of argument appeared again in Schleiermacher's preaching on the healing of the man born blind (John 9) and the raising of Lazarus (John 11).

John 11 and 12 each posed interpretive challenges for Schleiermacher's view of miracles, because the Johannine text appears to link belief to a miraculous event.[31] Schleiermacher refused to allow the faith of the disciples to rest upon either miracle, arguing that the Gospel had indicated that they already had faith prior to the miracle. Jesus' words in John 11, according to Schleiermacher, indicated that he knew the raising of Lazarus would strengthen the trust of the disciples that Jesus' words concerning his own death would be fulfilled, just as his words concerning Lazarus were fulfilled.[32] The miracle would bolster the disciples' fully formed faith through the testing of it that lay ahead. The nature of Schleiermacher's argument makes a clear distinction between the ground of faith and what might serve to strengthen it against trials. Similarly, in his interpretation of the voice from heaven in John 12, Schleiermacher argued that the disciples had to have had faith prior to hearing the voice.[33] In fact, their faith made it possible for them to hear and understand the voice when others did not.

Jesus also periodically exhibits miraculous knowledge in John, such as knowing the number of husbands of the Samaritan woman at the well (John 4) or Nathanael's nature prior to meeting him (John 1). Schleiermacher did not explain, nor even try to explain, what appears to be Jesus' miraculous knowledge. That which is beyond human explanation in the biblical text Schleiermacher did not attempt to explain. Neither did he attempt to deny occurrence of such events. Miracles are neither an ob-

30. SW II/8:424–25 (John 6:27–35 31.10.1824 P392).

31. See John 11:14–15, where Jesus is quoted: "Lazarus is dead. For your sake I am glad I was not there, so that you may believe." See also John 12:30 where Jesus says after a voice is heard from heaven, "This voice has come for your sake, not for mine."

32. SW II/9:253 (John 11:15–27 20.11.1825 P414).

33. SW II/9:341 (John 12:27–36 12.2.1826 P420). A peculiar feature of this sermon is Schleiermacher's contention that John may have provided only the sense of the voice from heaven but not the precise words. This contrasts with his argument in other sermons that John gives the precise words of Jesus. Compare SW II/9:283 (John 11:41–54 18.12.1825 P416). Schleiermacher did not say explicitly why he thought John would be more precise in his record of Jesus' speech than in his record of God's speech.

stacle to, nor a support for, faith. That made them relatively uninteresting to Schleiermacher as he preached.

Nicodemus

It appears that the discourse with Nicodemus in John 3:1–21 was primarily of interest to Schleiermacher early in his preaching career. With the exception of the sermon series, the sermons after 1812 used only individual verses from this pericope, which, when taken out of context, related to the liturgical day or season.[34]

Schleiermacher provided a sympathetic interpretation of Nicodemus as a leader in Israel who had come within Jesus' sphere of influence. John 3 was described by Schleiermacher as a compact statement of the Redeemer's understanding of new birth. This compactness was interpreted as a necessity due to the late hour at which the discourse occurred.[35] Although the Johannine text sets up a dialogue between Jesus and Nicodemus in which the latter expresses misunderstandings of what Jesus says, Schleiermacher consistently suggested that Nicodemus did not completely misunderstand.[36] The faith that Nicodemus expresses in the Johannine text was considered by Schleiermacher to be incomplete because it was founded upon the signs and wonders Jesus performed. This distinguished Nicodemus from the disciples received by Jesus in John 1.[37] However, Schleiermacher portrayed Nicodemus as being instructed by Jesus and learning from answers to the leading questions he had asked Jesus. The Johannine text does not require this reading; it reflects the operation of Schleiermacher's presupposition that persons who enter into the sphere of Jesus' influence come to recognize him as the Redeemer.

The Woman at the Well

Schleiermacher also preached on the pericope that describes an encounter between Jesus and a woman of Samaria at Jacob's well (John 4:1–42) in three different time periods at Trinity Church. His interpretation of the passage was significantly different in 1812, 1824, and 1832. What is

34. Verse 3:6 on the Spirit was used on Pentecost in 1828, verses 3:14–15 on Moses raising the serpent and the Son of Man being lifted up were used on Good Friday in 1826, and verses 3:20–21 on coming to the light were used during Christmastide in 1821.

35. SW II/8:159 (John 3:1–6 30.11.1823 P373).

36. SW II/1:499 (John 3:1–8 24.5.1812 P41) and SW II/8:160–161 (John 3:1–6 30.11.1823 P373).

37. SW II/8:158 (John 3:1–6 30.11.1823 P373).

striking is that the presupposition behind the 1824 and 1832 interpretations remained the same, even though the interpretations of the woman's response to Jesus are incompatible with each other.

The sermon from 1812 was one of the political sermons preached during the occupation of Berlin by the French.[38] The Johannine text functioned as a springboard or metaphor for the three points of the sermon. Jacob's well, at which Jesus meets the Samaritan woman, was discussed as an anchor for the *Volk,* which predated the division of Israel and Judah. This led to consideration of how a consciousness of *Volk* contributes to the well-being of a people. Schleiermacher was constructing the conception of *Volk* for the congregation. The second point considered the disastrous situation of a divided *Volk.* The third point concerned self-revelation and the conditions under which it was advisable. It was in the last point that Schleiermacher considered the role of Jesus' self-revelation in eliciting the woman's faith.

In this 1812 sermon, however, the emphasis of Schleiermacher's discussion was not the faith of the woman. Rather, he attended to the conditions of Jesus' self-revelation in order to encourage his congregation to be wise, but also to speak their hearts to one another. Under occupation public declarations and humor were risky, but Schleiermacher was concerned that his congregants would lose the ability to speak to one another from the heart if they did not do so in private. He used Jesus' self-revelation as a model for judicious decision-making about when to speak. This sermon did not link community to redemption, but it did demonstrate a keen concern for the survival of intimate trustworthy relations, which are the foundation of community. It is an antecedent to the presupposition that redemption leads to incorporation into Christian community.

The focus had shifted in the five sermons of 1824 away from Jesus' self-revelation to the faith of the woman.[39] It was the condition of the woman's partial faith that elicited Jesus' claim to Messiahship: "I am he." In contrast to the declaration that was requested by the skeptical and denied to them, and in contrast to the believing disciples who were told to remain silent about what they knew, Schleiermacher typified the woman as open to the truth and hope-filled in expectation of the Messiah. Her recognition of Jesus as a prophet made it possible for her to receive Jesus'

38. SW II/1:400–413 (John 4:4–26 19.1.1812 P34).

39. SW II/8:232–48 (John 4:1–10 1.2.1824 P379); SW II/8:249–62 (John 4:11–19 15.2.1824 P380); SW II/8:263–78 (John 4:20–24 14.3.1824 P381); SW II/8:279–90 (John 4:25–34 28.3.1824 P382); SW II/8:291–302 (John 4:35–42 11.4.1824 P383).

self-revelation in faith. The revelation matured a nascent faith; it focused and named what the woman already saw. Thus, the presupposition that it is obvious that Jesus is the Redeemer was protected in this reading of the story by describing the woman as recognizing the distinctiveness of Jesus. It was this recognition prior to Jesus' self-revelation that made possible her reception of the revelation. The woman saw Jesus as the Redeemer and merely needed permission to use the name Messiah for him.

In these sermons the woman was an example of the development of full faith in Jesus as the Redeemer. Contrary evidence in the biblical text was carefully interpreted in these sermons. Schleiermacher denied that the woman really could have misunderstood Jesus and taken him literally when she asked for the living water of which he spoke. Jesus would not have spoken to her in the manner in which he spoke if she was not capable of understanding.[40] This interpretation was consistent with Schleiermacher's interpretation of the Nicodemus story, and he made explicit reference to that story. The woman's request for living water meant: If it is the case that you have a spiritual good to give, give it to me, so that I can avoid the laboriousness of the law.[41] Schleiermacher's interpretation of the woman's response showed that the woman recognized Jesus as the Redeemer. She was also a positive example in the next sermon, in which she inquired about Jesus' view of an important religious question, even though he was a Jew and she was a Samaritan.[42] The sermon addressed the problem of religious differences within the faith and lauded the woman's desire to understand across difference as the factor that made possible the entire town's coming to faith in the Redeemer.[43] Mention of the woman's role as witness anticipated the following sermon, in which the woman took a step in faith and Jesus drew her further by identifying himself as the Messiah.[44] According to Schleiermacher, she was imitating his indirection when she suggested to the other villagers that they investigate for themselves if he were the Christ. Her role as a witness was honored but circumscribed in an excursus in the sermon that discussed the importance of women as believers within the realm of the household and the influencing of children. In the final sermon on this passage in the series Schleiermacher concluded that the Samaritan woman must have had a good reputation in the village

40. SW II/8:251 (John 4:11–19 15.2.1824 P380).

41. SW II/8:259.

42. SW II/8:263–78 (John 4:20–24 14.3.1824 P381).

43. SW II/8:264–65.

44. SW II/8:279–90 (John 4:25–34 28.3.1824 P382).

because her word was so influential.[45] This conclusion simplified the more complex situation suggested by the details of the biblical story.

This positive picture of the Samaritan woman was contradicted in one sermon on the entire pericope preached in January 1832.[46] The entire first section of this sermon interpreted the conversation between the Samaritan woman and Jesus in order to establish that Jesus could not have expected much from the conversation. Her failing is based not upon her moral standing but rather upon her decision not to respond directly and positively to what Jesus said. Her question to the villagers, "Can this be the Christ?" was read in this sermon as evidence of doubt (rather than an invitation, as in the 1824 sermons). Moreover, Jesus' request that she go get her husband was taken as evidence that it was clear to Jesus that she was not going to choose to comprehend the spiritual meaning behind his words. In this sermon the woman was a negative example.

What is consistent between these two very different interpretations of the biblical text is the presupposition that the woman should have recognized Jesus as the Redeemer. In 1824 she was taken to be a positive example because she did. In 1832 she was a negative example because she chose not to recognize or respond to what is evident. In the person of Jesus, in his words and presence, the Redeemer is apparent, whether or not an individual chooses to recognize it and respond.

At the Pool of Bethesda

The story of the healing of the lame man at the pool of Bethesda in John 5 is of interest because in the biblical text Jesus seeks out the man twice, once for healing and later for instruction. And yet, in spite of Jesus' attention to him, the healed man betrayed Jesus by identifying him to the Pharisees as having healed on the Sabbath. This account does not easily fit Schleiermacher's presupposition that it is apparent that Jesus is the Redeemer. The first problem is: If it were evident that Jesus was the Redeemer, people should have been seeking him rather than vice versa. Precisely this issue occupied Schleiermacher in his 1824 series sermon on this text.[47] Schleiermacher raised the question of why no one at the pool asked Jesus for healing, as if he were unknown, even though he had done many signs in Jerusalem.

45. SW II/8:291–302 (John 4:35–42 11.4.1824 P383).

46. SW II/3:169–80 (John 4:25–26 29.1.1832 P167). The two verses cited were used by Schleiermacher as a means of drawing attention to the entire biblical story.

47. SW II/8:320–21 (John 5:1–15 16.5.1824 P385).

The next problem is the miracle and its relation to the man's faith; in the Johannine text the miracle appears to evoke faith of some sort. Yet, according to Schleiermacher, the healed man in this pericope responded not with faith in Jesus as Redeemer, but only with faith in Jesus as a healer. In both the early (1794) and the series (1824) sermons Schleiermacher explained the combination of both healing and betrayal by suggesting that the man betrayed his own emerging faith by saying what was forbidden.[48] It was a betrayal because the man had partial faith, as evidenced by the healing, and therefore knew who Jesus was, but did not accept the discipleship that this knowledge placed before him. In 1824 Schleiermacher explained the source of this choice as vacillation between the perishable and the eternal, which prevents one from coming to a secure determination in relation to the eternal. This lack of secure determination makes it impossible for one to recognize the coherence of the earthly and heavenly.[49]

Recognizing Jesus as the Redeemer did not (and does not) guarantee a positive response to him. A series sermon on John 8:30–38 preached one year later reconsidered this issue. Schleiermacher argued that at the time of Jesus' life there was a beginning of faith that showed a potentiality for it; but it was incomplete because the expectations in it were mixed and not all of them corresponded to the true purpose God intended to achieve in Christ. Because these expectations were mixed, it was possible to have doubts about their fulfillment, and faith was lost in these doubts.[50] This confusion of expectations parallels Schleiermacher's description of the man healed at the pool of Bethesda. The man retained his mixed expectations and consequently denied the faith in which he had been healed. Schleiermacher's interpretation protected his presupposition. That is, although it was apparent to the healed man that Jesus is the Redeemer, he had turned away from what he knew.

Lord, to Whom Shall We Go?

By 1824, the confession of Peter in John 6:68 was a refrain that Schleiermacher used to express both the emotive and the didactic content of faith in Christ: "Lord, to whom shall we go? You have the words of eternal life." What was evoked in this quote was the naiveté of a faith the foundation of which is apparent. Schleiermacher used the confessional quote

48. SW II/7:292 (John 5:5–16 1794 *Trinitatiszeit* P332).
49. SW II/8:320–21 (John 5:1–15 16.5.1824 P385).
50. SW II/9:98 (John 8:30–38 15.5.1825 P403).

most frequently in his conclusions, often as the final sentence.[51] It is the word that should echo in persons of faith, just as it is the word which echoed in the sanctuary in the transition between the sermon and the rest of the liturgy. The confession was used as an emblem for what was taken to be readily apparent both to the first disciples and to the congregation to whom Schleiermacher preached. There is no other source of redemption and eternal life.

Only once in the sermons available today did Schleiermacher find it necessary to elaborate on the meanings expressed by the scriptural verse. That occurred in the early morning sermon on John 6:61–71, a part of the John series.

> Nevertheless, the testimony that Peter gives here is the one that everyone must be able to repeat in the innermost ground of their hearts if the word of the Lord is life in them, and they have understood that Christ was sent from God to bring the bread of heaven.[52]

Even in his explanation of the biblical text, Schleiermacher did not attempt to show in what way Peter's confession was true. Its truth was apparent to those who were in the sphere of Jesus' influence. Rather, Schleiermacher's response to the text was to use it as a model for behavior that responds to the Redeemer with faith. It was assumed that we can see and know what the first disciples saw and knew, and that the experience is sufficient for faith in Jesus.

The Man Born Blind

The Johannine story of the healing of the man born blind (John 9:1–41) was problematic for Schleiermacher on several counts. He did not preach on the text, according to our records, until three sermons in the John series in 1825, and then only once thereafter, in 1832.[53] Schleiermacher found it necessary to account for why Jesus needed to name himself as Messiah, also for how the man came to be healed prior to any expression

51. For examples, see SW II/8:364 (John 5:24–30 27.6.1824 P387); SW II/8:379 (John 5:31–40 11.7.1824 P388); SW II/9:222 (John 10:22–33 9.10.1825 P411); SW II/3:10 (John 14:27 12.6.1831 P140); and SW II/3:131 (John 16:27 11.12.1831 P162). SW II/3:472 (John 13:34 10.2.1833 P199) is an unusual case, in that the verse is used as part of the argument for one of the main points of the sermon.

52. SW II/8:473–4 (John 6:61–71 9.1.1825 P396).

53. SW II/9:138–52 (John 9:1–7 17.7.1825 P406); SW II/9:153–67 (John 9:8–23 31.7.1825 P407); SW II/9:168–83 (John 9:24–41 14.8.1825 P408); SW II/3:181–94 (John 9:35–38 12.2.1832 P168).

of faith, including any request for healing. Arguing from textual silence, Schleiermacher described the blind man as having chosen not to have faith in Jesus as the Redeemer. Jesus had passed that way and passed by the man often, so the man must have recognized him. The man's silence when he might have asked for healing was an expression of his decision against faith, according to Schleiermacher. This argument only makes sense if it was obvious who Jesus was—the Redeemer.

In Schleiermacher's interpretation, the man's choice against faith was transformed by events precipitated by the question asked by the disciples concerning the cause of the man's blindness. Jesus placed mud on the man's eyes and required a faith decision from him, a decision in the form of following his directions for washing the mud off. This action indicated that the man believed Jesus could heal him. After the healing, the faith of the man was still partial—he described Jesus as a prophet. It was to complete this partial faith that Jesus sought him out later. In the second encounter Jesus invited belief in himself as Son of God.[54] The meaning of the question of invitation ("Do you believe in the Son of God?") was elaborated in a sermon preached several weeks later in the series. "That is to say, do you feel in yourself a desire that one should come down from above with higher gifts than all of those which have until now delighted you? And if such a one comes, do you intend to avail yourself of his help and follow him?"[55]

Belief in Jesus as the Son of God was particularly important, according to Schleiermacher, because the Jewish community had cast the blind man out. He would have remained outside all community unless he developed faith in Jesus as the Redeemer, the faith with which one enters Christian community. The Johannine text does not mention the healed man's incorporation into community; it only shows Jesus seeking out and speaking to the man a second time. Schleiermacher clearly presupposed that incorporation into Christian community was a vital consequence of redemptive relationship to the Redeemer, and he brought this presupposition to the text.

54. The Johannine text Schleiermacher read with this sermon read the textual variant "Son of God." More recent critical editions of John prefer the more difficult reading "Son of Man."

55. SW II/9:187 (John 10:1–11 28.8.1825 P409).

The Farewell Discourses

In his preaching on the farewell discourses (John 13–17), Schleiermacher emphasized the theme of love. Love of God was connected to human relationships in all stages of Schleiermacher's preaching career. One of his earliest sermons on these chapters, a 1795 outline on John 16:14, explicitly linked the "Fatherhood" of God with our love of one another and our helping one another.[56] The 1797 outline on John 13:35 expands this to people's relation to the world. Its theme states that, "the spirit of love is the spirit of the discipleship of Christ."[57] The third and closing point relates this love well beyond a purely personal relationship to Christ: "One cannot be useful to the world without love."[58] The implication is that discipleship includes being useful to the world.

Even when the stated preaching text does not mention love, Schleiermacher had it in mind. In 1797, 1802 and 1806 he preached on John 15:15 (you are no longer servants, but friends). The 1802 outline explicitly names love as being presupposed, as an act in which friends of Christ engage.[59] The 1806 outline devotes half the sermon to the contrast between love and fear as the difference between servants and friends, although only love of God is mentioned in the outline.[60] The earliest outline of the three, from 1797, does not mention love explicitly, but it concludes the second half by stating that to become friends of God we must do what God commands us.[61] The command to which this most likely refers occurs three verses earlier in John 15:12 : "love one another as I have loved you." Without using 15:12 as the preaching text, all three outlines keep it in peripheral view.

A community founded upon this mutual love appears to be presupposed in the early preaching on the discourses. It is explicitly named in the mature preaching, particularly in the 1830s.

56. SN 51 (Akademie der Wissenschaften, Berlin) 63 (John 16:14 25.5.1795 also published see P493) "Hier zeigt sich Gott als Vater der da alle[n] wo[h]l will und will dass seine Kinder sich lieben und sich unter einander aushelfen sollen."

57. SN 52 (Akademie der Wissenschaften, Berlin) 46 (John 13:35 14.10.1797) "Thema: Geist der Liebe ist Geist der Jüngenschaft Christi." (This is my reading of the manuscript.)

58. SN 52.46 "3. Man kann der Welt nicht nüzlich seyn ohne Liebe."

59. Bauer, *Patriotischer Prediger*, 324 (John 15:15 16.8.1802 P555).

60. Bauer, *Patriotischer Prediger*, 326–27 (John 15:9, 14–15 17.8.1806 P16). This sermon was also published as a full transcription in SW II/1:208–22. I have referred to the outline because it is in Schleiermacher's hand (Bauer transcribed SN 56:4), and because the point is more succinct in the outline.

61. Bauer, *Patriotischer Prediger*, 323 (John 15:15 28.5.1797 P554).

> He [Jesus] had come to originate a new common life, not only to bind each individual to himself, but also all with one another, with the love with which he loved everyone: That is the single command which he gave them, which is also the expression, indeed it alone is the complete expression of the purpose which he wanted to achieve, for which purpose he had come.[62]

This purpose for which the Redeemer came was to offer eternal life. What constituted eternal life was stated both indirectly and directly in Schleiermacher's preaching on John.

> That he was the life they knew; but now he wanted to secure them in the conviction concerning the life that he had imparted to them through faith in him, and in this manner: that he presented the command to love to them not as an external law, but he had rather breathed into them as an ever lively impulse that this [command] is eternal life.[63]

Faith in the Redeemer is secured through the impulse to love one another as we have been loved. This command to love is eternal life. The community formed of those who love is critical for the faith, not only for what it does actively but simply through its existence as a community that loves.

It is not clear in these sermons on the farewell discourses when redemption that was initiated by direct encounter with Jesus during his life was complete. The late sermons read as if incorporation into the faith community around Jesus was the concluding, or at least decisive, part of a process of redemption. In other words, redemption includes and depends upon the person of faith entering into an intimate community founded upon and actively expressing the Redeemer's love.[64] The early sermon outlines on the farewell discourses certainly explore the relationship between love of the Redeemer and love of others, but they do not connect this love directly to a community. Neither do the early sermon outlines appear to relate the love of others by a persons of faith directly to redemption. While the interest in community and the relationships that make it possible are found in the early sermons, linkage between community and redemption seems to have developed later as a presupposition behind Schleiermacher's interpretation of the farewell discourses.

62. SW II/3:233 (John 16:33 8.4.1832 P173).
63. SW II/9:426 (John 14:1–6 4.5.1826 P426).
64. SW II/3:472 (John 13:34 10.2.1833 P199).

Jesus' Death

Schleiermacher often used texts from portions of John outside the Passion and Resurrection narratives to discuss the Passion, Resurrection and Ascension. Two Johannine sermons from 1795 and 1796 in Landsberg concern the role of Jesus' death in Christian faith. The first of these, preached in May 1795, began with the text from John 16:14: "He [the Spirit of Truth] will glorify me, because he will take what is mine and declare it to you." This text was used as an occasion to list all that Schleiermacher believed was made clear in Jesus' teachings and in his dignity as teacher and example. Each sub-point of the outline contrasts two versions of doctrines, the second of which is explained.[65] What Schleiermacher said in the outline concerning substitutionary atonement contrasts this doctrine with the death of Jesus considered as an expression of love:

> I. 1) the [teaching], that God is the Father of all people.
>
> d) In contrast to the punishment, which must be satisfied through the death of Jesus, in which God appears unjust and unfatherly toward Christ: the teaching that he allowed the death of Jesus, because without it the instruction of people could not occur. Here God shows himself as Father who desires good for all and desires that his children love him and commands them to help one another.[66]

The outline is not clear about why Jesus' death was necessary for the instruction of humanity, but it clearly rejects substitutionary theories as explanations and turns to divine love as the central factor in divine activity.[67]

That the work of Jesus is brought to an end by his death is made manifest in the outline for the Good Friday service in 1796.[68] The text

65. Zimmer, "erster Amtsthätigkeit," 369–71 and SN 51 (Akademie der Wissenschaften, Berlin) 62–63 (John 16:14 25.5.1795 P493). Unfortunately, Zimmer's transcription of the manuscript omits the statements of explanation of Schleiermacher's position in several places, and sometimes it includes errors in what is included.

66. SN 51 (Akademie der Wissenschaften, Berlin) 63. This is my reading of the manuscript, which varies in minor points from Zimmer's transcription: "I. 1) die [Lehre], dass Gott der Vater aller Menschen ist. d) Im Gegensatz von der Strafgerechtigkeit, die durch den Tod Jesu befriedigt werden müsste, wo Gott ungerecht und unväterlich gegen Christum erscheint: die Lehre, dass er den Tod Jesu um des willen zugelassen [habe], weil ohne ihn die Belehrung der Menschen nicht stattfinden konnte. Hier zeigt sich Gott als Vater der da alle[n] wol will und will dass seine Kinder sich lieben und sich unter einander aushelfen sollen".

67. The later explanation Schleiermacher provided in his preaching was that Jesus' death made unmistakably evident that redemption is first of all spiritual.

68. SN 51 (Akademie der Wissenschaften, Berlin), 111–12, and Zimmer, "erster Amt-

was the Johannine report of Jesus' words from the cross: "It is finished." In Schleiermacher's interpretation, Jesus' death brought his work to an end; the death itself was not a part of the work. The two parts of Jesus' work are the same as those of every human being: self-formation (the work of a life in itself) and the particular individual's part in God's plan. Both parts of Jesus' work were complete at the moment he spoke on the cross. Schleiermacher's conclusion was that such an end is worthy of envy and should be sought.

These two early outlines do not precisely indicate what was included in Schleiermacher's theological position, but they do make clear that while Jesus' death may have been a consequence of his work, it was not part of the work itself. Jesus' redeeming work occurred prior to his death. While these sermon outlines reflect this presupposition, it became clearer in later sermons on John.

The next occasions available to us when Schleiermacher's preaching on John addressed the crucifixion were his Good Friday sermons at Trinity Church, Berlin in 1809 and 1810. The 1809 sermon was preached in a climate of impending war, which began within days in April 1809.[69] It was in this decisive round of fighting beginning in 1809 that Prussia began to use non-professional soldiers for the first time. This sermon contributed to the acceptance of the idea of ordinary men fighting and risking death. The text from John 10:17–18 concerns Jesus' discussion of his power to lay down his life and to take it up again. The sermon was built around the idea of living to lose one's life. Hearers were urged to recognize their own ability to live with the same consciousness the Redeemer had, that is, conviction of their power to lay down their lives. Yet, what is redemptive is not the death itself but rather the consciousness with which one lives, willing to die. Schleiermacher discussed this in the scriptural terms of persons of faith being raised by the Redeemer to himself only as they take up their cross and follow him. What is critical for our faith is the Redeemer's way of living in the face of death, not the death itself. The crucifixion is necessary only so that the God-consciousness of the Redeemer is clearly a consciousness that is sustained in the face of death. That is to say, the Redeemer's consciousness exists in freedom even under the greatest duress. This sermon interpreted the Redeemer's death as important insofar as it was a reflection of his life.

sthätigkeit," 371–72 (John 19:30 25.3.1796 P495). Zimmer has omissions.

69. SW II/4:778–81 (John 10:17–18 31.3.1809 P30).

The same theme was repeated in another form in the Good Friday sermon the following year, 1810.[70] Returning to the text "It is finished," Schleiermacher repeated his interpretation that the Redeemer's death secured his teaching.[71] It did this by placing the spiritual before the physical and sensate. The Redeemer's death separates those who believe in an earthly savior and salvation from those who believe in the Redeemer's real purpose—to bring eternal life. The death does not add to the redemption, it simply confirms a true understanding of it.

The death of the Redeemer confirms that redemption is not earthly or perishable but is a matter of the eternal. However, eternal, here, is not a future time discontinuous with present time and experience. Eternal life is a potential present—a potential fulfilled in the Redeemer and experienced by those who believe in him. It is a life of the spirit, in contrast to a life of pure impressionable sensation.[72] This eternal life is available only through the Redeemer. Genuine persons of faith, that is, those who understand the spiritual nature of redemption through Christ, are separated by the crucifixion from those who sought an earthly savior. This construction implies that persons of faith are genuinely so prior to the crucifixion. In particular, crucifixion reveals true and false belief, rather than its being a part of the content of true belief.

When Schleiermacher preached the John series in 1823–27, he used traditional language about redemption more frequently. So, in 1824 he is recorded as having said:

> If the Lord had through his Son then sought such worshippers in spirit and in truth, we may not forget that he could not have sought and found them apart from having given his earthly life in death.[73]

However, justification for this claim for the role of the Redeemer's death is not provided by the sermon, nor does it appear to be a natural consequence of the larger argument. A careful reading suggests that Schleiermacher had added to the list of consequences that follow from the Redeemer's death, but he had not changed his picture of the Redeemer's effectiveness prior to his death: Redemption was experienced by genuine persons of faith prior to the crucifixion.

70. SW II/7:383–390 (John 19:30 20.4.1810 P339).
71. SW II/7:388.
72. Ibid.
73. SW II/8:277 (John 4:20–24 14.3.1824 P381).

In the series sermons and later, Schleiermacher described the death of the Redeemer as necessary for propagation of the faith. This idea appears in several forms, the most common of which is the metaphor of a grain of wheat dying in order to bear fruit, a metaphor found in John 12:24. The reference is usually general; that is, Schleiermacher assumed that the hearer knew to what the "seed" refers.[74] On most occasions the focus of Schleiermacher's interpretation was upon the disappearance of the seed in order for a harvest to occur. From that perspective the seed is the physical presence of the Redeemer. The physical life of the Redeemer ended in order that his effectiveness would not be limited to those who could meet him in the flesh. In contrast, in 1824 the Palm Sunday sermon in the series on John records a second interpretation:

> It is still the word of God, which came from his mouth; it is still the same light, which when the word became flesh, shone in the darkness in order to permeate it; that is what is sown in the minds and hearts (*Gemüther*) of all people, . . .[75]

This interpretation focuses upon the sowing and what is taken in by persons of faith, that is, the teaching and presence of the Redeemer. In this reading, death is not directly in view. Death comes into view in Schleiermacher's interpretation of the metaphor only to express the propagation of faith beyond the first disciples. The content of redemption itself is suggested in the second interpretation: The redeemed have taken the teaching and presence of the Redeemer into their hearts and minds.

The sermon series argues periodically for the importance of the death of the Redeemer for securing the spiritual nature of redemption and for propagation of the faith. The death is placed alongside the teaching and presence of the Redeemer as being salvific. It is significant that the argument here focuses on the role of the death, not on the role of the teaching. Schleiermacher assumed that his hearers accepted the role of the teaching as evident. It remained for him to remind or convince his congregation of the role of the Redeemer's death.

In 1832 the sermon for *Rogate* reflected the supporting role for the crucifixion in Schleiermacher's view of God's larger plan. The sermon used the occasion to consider what had been gained from Christ in the previ-

74. For examples see: SW II/8:290 (John 4:25–34 28.3.1824 P382); SW II/9:327 (John 12:20–26 5.2.1826 P419); SW II/3:481 (John 13:34 10.2.1833 P199); SW II/9:477–78 (John 15:1–7 2.7.1826 P430).

75. SW II/8:299 (John 4:35–42 11.4.1824 P383).

ous year, which required knowing what to expect.[76] Schleiermacher identified two things we may expect: that Christ will bring a lively perception (*Anschauung*) of his and our Father in heaven, and that Christ will dwell in us just as he dwells in the Father. The crucifixion was addressed under the first point. Our focus, according to this sermon, ought to be upon Christ's love in his suffering. Christ's love makes evident the Father's love. An 1821 sermon on Jesus' word from the cross, "I thirst," also demonstrates this focus of interpretation.[77] Rather than being an expression of need, the words were an offer to the soldiers of opportunity for compassion. In the expression of such compassion the relationship of enmity between soldiers and Christ would have been transcended. Thus, to the end, the Redeemer was providing the setting for potential redemption, even of his enemies. This loving act of the Redeemer is in continuity with his entire earlier ministry. Events of the crucifixion are only part of the larger pattern of God's love. Jesus' death brings into sharper focus the significant themes of his work: a reordering of life in which a person of faith is one with Christ, in which the spiritual transforms the physical, and in which love of God and of one another is the operating mode for life.[78]

Resurrection

The Resurrection as an event was not a central theme in Schleiermacher's preaching on Johannine texts. He preached on the verses describing the empty tomb and appearance to Mary Magdalene five times. Two of these sermons were on John 20:17 ("I am ascending to my Father and your Father"). Of these two, the only existing outline, for a 1797 sermon, uses the text as an Ascension text.[79] So, the Johannine version of the empty tomb itself was used only three times by Schleiermacher: in 1795, 1796 and in the 1827 series sermon.[80] Of these, the only sermon available to

76. SW II/3:265–75 (John 14:9 27.5.1832 P177).

77. SW II/4:293–306 (John 19:28–29 8.4.1821 P67).

78. This reading of Schleiermacher's preaching on John contradicts Emanuel Hirsch's description of Schleiermacher's position. Hirsch, relying particularly on the *Life of Jesus* lectures, argues that Schleiermacher interpreted the crucifixion as the end of the old human Gestalt and the beginning of a new way of being human. Hirsch, *Schleiermachers Christusglaube,* 92. However, the crucifixion does not play this central a role in Schleiermacher's preaching on John.

79. SN 52 (Akademie der Wissenschaften, Berlin), 27–28 and Zimmer, "erster Amtsthätigkeit," 374–75 (John 20:17 25.5.1797 P498) and a diary notation: "John 20:17 11.4.1830 Easter".

80. Bauer mentions the first sermon (John 20:4ff 19.4.1795); SN 51 (Akademie der Wissenschaften, Berlin) 114–15 (John 20:1–10 28.3.1796); diary notation: "John 20:1–

us is a 1796 manuscript outline. Whether this absence of sermons on the text is an accident of transmission or a result of the relative unimportance Schleiermacher placed upon this text, we cannot know.

We do, however, have many sermons on the Resurrection appearance stories in John 20 and 21. He preached on some part of these two chapters on at least 43 occasions—with one exception, always during Eastertide.[81] One of the earliest of these sermons, from 1795 in Landsberg, suggests that the idea of Resurrection was problematic for Schleiermacher.[82] The sermon outline addresses religious faith in the context of the faith persons have in their experience and in their reason. Schleiermacher had Jesus' death and Resurrection in view as problematic, which made faith itself problematic. He responded to the problem by affirming the familiar nature of faith, but he did not attempt in the outline to explain either Jesus' death or Resurrection.

As we have seen, Schleiermacher did explain the Redeemer's death as he continued to preach on John. He did not, however, either explain the Resurrection or deny it in his preaching on John. The presence of the Redeemer in the appearance stories was treated in the same way as in all the accounts of his appearances prior to the passion. The Redeemer experienced complete continuity between his earlier life and his resurrected life.[83] The ambiguity in the Johannine account of Ascension concerning whether or not a physical event occurred allowed Schleiermacher similar ambiguity concerning what happened physically at the Resurrection, even while a spiritual reality was explicitly affirmed: The Redeemer was present to persons of faith.

At least some of Schleiermacher's mature preaching intentionally placed less importance upon Resurrection appearances than the Johannine text itself implies. The series sermon on John 14:18–24, preached in 1826, explicitly denied that Jesus' promise, "I will come to you," refers to the Resurrection appearances. The reasoning was straightforward and was based upon the first half of the sentence: "I will not leave you orphaned." Jesus could not possibly have had the Resurrection appearances in mind

18 15.4.1827 Easter".

81. The exception was his last recorded John sermon, on New Year's Day 1834 on John 20:19 (SW II/3:752–64, P233); trans., Lawler, *Fifteen Sermons*, 258–77. This sermon is unusual not only in its text but also in its style. Schleiermacher spoke directly to the congregation concerning their life together without using biblical examples, as was his normal practice. He was quite ill from pneumonia at the time and died of it six weeks later.

82. SN 51 (Akademie der Wissenschaften, Berlin), 54–5 and Bauer, *Ungedruckte Predigten*, 104–6 (John 20:24ff 19.4.1795 P581).

83. SW II/9:417f (John 14:1–6 4.5.1826 P426).

here, according to Schleiermacher, because they were temporary events that could not give substance to the promise not to leave persons of faith orphaned.[84] The Christian community, as it evidences the love of God made manifest in the Redeemer, fulfills the promise. Two months later, preaching on John 16:16–23, Schleiermacher repeated this interpretation in his discussion of the promise, "in a little while you will not see me, and then you will see me." Neither this promise nor the comparison to childbirth in this text refers to Resurrection appearances, because the Resurrection appearances are short-lived. Instead, what is born is the church, which will not cease.[85] Although Schleiermacher preached again on texts surrounding these two, these two series sermons are the only sermons on these texts of which we have a record. Both shift the fulfillment of Jesus' promises away from the Resurrection and onto the Christian community upon which the church is founded.

Concern for Christian communities is particularly evident in Schleiermacher's preaching on the Resurrection appearances. As early as 1796 he urged his hearers to express their religious convictions, for two reasons: to confirm the convictions of others, and to instruct or correct (*Belehrung*) others through discussion.[86] Community depends upon these expressions for its existence. Two characteristics of community were more clearly specified in his 1812 sermon on John 21. In community one finds small circles in which the distinctive nature (*Wesen*) of an individual can emerge and be influential, and one finds enjoyment of one another in thankfulness and grace.[87] The theme of this sermon summarized the picture: "the gathering of the disciples with one another and the Redeemer as the proper example for our intimate relations with one another."[88]

The importance Schleiermacher placed upon a faithful person's relationship to a faith community is highlighted by his interpretation of the dialogue between Jesus and Peter ("Do you love me? Feed my sheep.") Schleiermacher described Peter's reception of forgiveness for his denial of Jesus as an event occurring prior to this dialogue. Peter already loves Jesus, as he repeatedly affirms in the Johannine account. So, the purpose of the dialogue, according to Schleiermacher, was to bring Peter back into the spiritual life. The details were specified in a sermon from 1833.[89] Peter

84. SW II/9:445 (John 14:18–24 4.6.1826 P428).

85. SW II/9:524–36 (John 16:16–23 27.8.1826 P434).

86. SN 51 (Akademie der Wissenschaften, Berlin) 116–7 and Zimmer, "erster Amtsthätigkeit," 373–4 (John 20:19 3.4.1796 P497).

87. SW II/1:462–477 (John 21:2–23 12.4.1812 P39).

88. SW II/1:465.

89. SW II/3:546–47 (John 21:1–8 21.4.1833 P205).

had been forgiven when Jesus had appeared to him earlier. (Here Schleiermacher referred to Luke.) His sin no longer disturbed his relationship to the Redeemer. Yet, the matter of his re-incorporation into Christian community was still open, until the dialogue found in John 21 occurred. The Redeemer acted to restore Peter to full community. Schleiermacher linked this story to the community because of the centrality of love; as we have seen in his preaching on chapters 13–16, love is the connection between a person of faith and the Redeemer and the community.

Ascension

Schleiermacher preached on Johannine texts on Ascension Day at least five times and referred to the departure of the Redeemer as necessary for the development of faith in a number of other Johannine sermons. His basic interpretation of the Ascension remained consistent over thirty years. The Ascension was necessary in order that persons of faith would understand redemption as inner and spiritual rather than physical or based upon external authority. The truth is the fruit of inner conviction.[90] The Ascension makes possible present fulfillment of Jesus' promise "I am with you" and evokes "trust in the hope that we will be with Christ."[91] The texts of the Ascension sermons were most often from the discourses and highlight the promises Jesus made.[92]

In Schleiermacher's preaching on John, Jesus' death and Ascension seem to be more decisive events than the Resurrection for clarifying the true nature of faith. Jesus' death and Ascension necessitate a full faith relationship to the Redeemer, a relationship that was possible but not necessary so long as he was physically present. Schleiermacher emphasized the absence of the Redeemer in physical form as that which requires persons of faith to recognize faith as spiritual.

90. Bauer, *Ungedruckte Predigten,* 31 (John 16:5–7 14.5.1795 P568).

91. SN 53 (Akademie der Wissenschaften, Berlin), 114, and Zimmer, *Predigtenentwürfe,* 67 (John 17:24 22.5.1800 P545).

92. SN 51 (Akademie der Wissenschaften, Berlin), 60–61, and Bauer, *Ungedruckte Predigten,* 31–32 (John 16:5–7 14.5.1795 P568); SN 52, 27–28, and Zimmer, "erster Amtsthätigkeit," 374–75 (John 20:17 25.5.1797 P498); SN 53, 114, and Zimmer, *Predigtenentwürfe,* 67–68 (John 17:24 22.5.1800); SW II/9:417–27 (John 14:1–6 4.5.1826 P426) (part of the series sermons); diary notation: "John 16:28 15.5.1828 Frühpredigt."

Presuppositions

It is apparent to all who come into the sphere of Jesus' influence that he is the Redeemer.

Having surveyed the most significant pericopes in Schleiermacher's preaching on John, we turn directly to the presuppositions evident in this preaching. We are now in a position to clarify three terms in this first presupposition. The phrase "It is apparent" is intentionally vague about how persons recognize the Redeemer, because Schleiermacher acknowledged a variety of ways that persons encountered and responded to Jesus. There was not a particular act or teaching or event that everyone who responded positively or negatively to Jesus experienced. The complexity of Jesus himself interacted with each individual in question. From the accounts of Nathanael, Nicodemus, and the woman at the well, one would expect that a teaching conversation was the necessary condition for Jesus' identity to become apparent. This was the most frequent way described in Schleiermacher's preaching. He turned to the discourse and teaching texts in John more frequently than to the others, but the healing stories also were interpreted with this presupposition. The man born blind and the man at the pool at Bethesda were expected to be able to perceive enough about Jesus from his acts as a public healer and teacher to respond to him with at least initial faith. Such initial faith was described as partial, but it could be developed into a fuller faith. Moreover, it was Schleiermacher's expectation that persons who had heard about Jesus from a distance should have at least this initial faith. He explained the lack of this initial faith as a decision on the part of the individual. So, what is "apparent" has two degrees: what one saw and knew from a distance, hearing about Jesus and his teaching, and what one saw and knew by interacting personally with Jesus. From a distance it is apparent that one has the opportunity for fuller faith if one draws closer to Jesus. When one does draw closer into the sphere of Jesus' influence, it is apparent that he is more than a healer or a prophet; he is the Redeemer.

The line demarcating Jesus' sphere of influence was not sharply drawn by Schleiermacher in his preaching. It is a function of proximity, time, and degree of Jesus' attention. Schleiermacher interpreted Jesus' interactions with Nathanael, Nicodemus, and the woman at the well as bringing each of them into his sphere of influence, while he acknowledged that the length of these interactions was short. The group of men who became disciples, including Philip and John, spent a full day with Jesus, though not as the exclusive center of his attention, and that was sufficient for full faith. Persons who had had Jesus' direct attention, even if briefly, like the man healed at the pool of Bethesda, were faulted for choosing against faith. Jesus' direct attention to one's self put one within Jesus' sphere of influence, but so did a longer period in the larger circle of his followers.

Across his preaching career, as Schleiermacher came to emphasize the relational aspects of faith more, his preferred reference to Jesus became the name Redeemer. This name identifies Jesus as he is experienced by us, the one who redeems us. The offer is universal. The acceptance of redemption is not; acceptance of redemption is a choice. Schleiermacher described persons who were in a position to recognize and accept the Redeemer and did not do so. He interpreted this as a free decision not to accept the Redeemer and thereby not to accept redemption. Cognition of the Redeemer is not the problem. Acceptance is. The Johannine stories that were interpreted in this way were not Schleiermacher's favorite preaching texts. It was not a theme on which he dwelt often in his preaching on John, but it was present as a theme. The Redeemer, in Schleiermacher's preaching on John, is the one who "has the words of eternal life," the one in whom we have seen the "glory of the only Son of the Father," the one who gave us the command to love one another as he has loved us. We are redeemed by what the Redeemer has given to us, which we have received from him when we recognize and accept who he is.

Redemption is available through the Redeemer prior to his death and resurrection.

The operation of this second presupposition is most evident in two different parts of Schleiermacher's preaching on John: in his picture of the faith of the disciples during Jesus' lifetime and in his interpretation of the Crucifixion, Resurrection, and Ascension. Redemption is not a term Schleiermacher used often in his preaching on John. Instead, he described faith (*Glaube*) as though one who has full or living faith in the Redeemer has experienced redemption. Although Schleiermacher did not define redemption as such in these sermons, he consistently drew pictures of life reordered by faith in the Redeemer. The early sermon outlines tend to consider this reordering from an ethical perspective, that is to say, how we should act and sometimes how we should think.[93] The sermons after 1809 tend to consider this reordering more relationally, from the perspective of

93. This observation is not in agreement with the view of either Meier-Dorken or Tice, who critiques Meier-Dorken. See Meier-Dorken, *Die Theologie der frühen Predigten Schleiermachers,* and Tice, "Themes in Schleiermacher's Early Theology."

how we see ourselves and therefore relate to self and others as spiritual and physical beings.

From the beginning of his preaching on John, Schleiermacher described the life of faith to be a way of living in union with Christ and the will of God. A 1791 sermon on prayer described the prayer in the name of Jesus enjoined by the Johannine text as prayer in the manner of Jesus and for that for which he prayed.[94] The center of this prayer is laying open one's inner life to God's will. The description reveals a faith grounded in unity with Jesus. This description became more explicit and thematic as Schleiermacher preached across his career. One grows in unity with Christ and through him with the Father, which is to say, one grows in faith, but this growth is gradual. It was discussed in terms of friendship with God in one of the few university sermons at Halle:

> For friendship with God is, as holds good with every friendship, not an impassioned movement (*Bewegung*) that begins powerfully and thundering and thereafter wanes and disappears; rather, it begins with a pure turning of the heart to God, from which follow convergence and uniting only gradually.[95]

Schleiermacher preached in such a way as to move people along in the process of redemption and sanctification. He assumed that his listeners were in that process somewhere. It is difficult to define a clear boundary between redemption and sanctification on the basis of these sermons. On one of the rare occasions on which he indicated the relationship and used the term sanctification (*Heiligung*), Schleiermacher described a progression beginning with the turning of the heart to the Redeemer, which results in living faith. Then with this living faith the slow gradual work of sanctification begins.[96] This description suggests that redemption involves turning one's heart to the Redeemer and coming to living faith. That Schleiermacher viewed even this as a process rather than as an irrevocable moment was indicated by his interpretation of the story of the man healed at the pool of Bethesda. Beginning to turn to the Redeemer may be interrupted and the promise of full, living faith may remain unfulfilled.

With this understanding of redemption in mind, it is clear from Schleiermacher's characterization of the disciples that their faith is living or full faith prior to the crucifixion. This is especially evident in his interpretation of chapter one and in his repetition of Peter's exclamation "To

94. SW II/7:30 (John 16:23 29.5.1791 P311).
95. SW II/1:220 (John 15:9,14,15 17.8.1806 P16).
96. SW II/3:179 (John 4:25–26 29.1.1832 P167).

whom shall we go? You have the words of eternal life." The trust in the impression Jesus made upon the disciples, and their knowledge of his glory as the only Son of the Father, which Schleiermacher ascribed to them on the day of their encounter with Jesus, are the features he regularly used to describe living faith. Furthermore, Schleiermacher regularly used Peter's words from the middle of the Johannine account of Jesus' ministry as a confession of his congregation's post-Resurrection faith. This suggests strongly that the faith Peter expressed was not surpassed by the events of the Crucifixion, Resurrection, and Ascension.

The Redeemer's death was important because it reflected the work of his life and confirmed that redemption is not earthly or perishable but is eternal. This is confirmation of what was already available and evident in the work of the Redeemer. The Resurrection was addressed primarily through the Resurrection appearances, which also served to confirm the spiritual nature of the redemption made possible by encounter with the Redeemer. The Ascension did not add substance to the faith but loosened any dependence of believers upon physical location, further underscoring redemption as an inner work. Schleiermacher interpreted each of these events as re-inscribing what was already present and available in the Redeemer's ministry prior to the passion.

Redemption is directly associated with incorporation into a community of Christians.

The community of believers that Schleiermacher presupposed was not identical with the institutional church viewed either as a denomination or as a congregation. The communities that he suggested exist within these institutions are more intimate associations the boundaries of which are informal rather than formal. As we saw in the discussion of Schleiermacher's preaching on the farewell discourses, there was some ambiguity in his preaching about the relationship between redemption and incorporation into Christian community. There is no doubt that incorporation is closely related to redemption. The question is whether incorporation is a part of redemption itself, or whether it follows as a critical result of redemption. This question is left unanswered in the sermons for two reasons. First, it requires definition of terms in a doctrinal context, and creating such a context would have interfered with the purpose of the preaching itself, that is, to present the faith as a living experience in which those assembled share and might share more deeply. Second, the first disciples came into the sphere of Christ's influence, experienced redemption, and then were drawn by him into community; but later persons of faith come into the sphere of Christ's influence only in the context of Christian community. So, for later persons of faith redemption occurs in the context of community. This was clearly not the case for many of the persons who encountered Christ during his lifetime, and yet Schleiermacher was quite clear in saying that the redemption experienced by both groups is the same. For both groups redemption is directly associated with incorporation into community.

In Schleiermacher's preached presentation of Christian faith, the experience of relationship to the Redeemer was always closely associated with incorporation into a community of Christians. Whether or not the Johannine text suggests it, Schleiermacher consistently described persons who come to faith as being led directly into community. When this did not occur, it was because individuals had betrayed their potential faith (as in the case of the man healed at the pool of Bethesda).

In his dissertation on Schleiermacher's early preaching Kurt Jung argued that for Schleiermacher the integration of an individual into the community was the completion of redemption.[97] Because of his choice of sources for the early sermons, Jung did not read many sermons on Johannine texts. His primary source for his point was an 1800 sermon on Acts 17:24–27.[98] It is less clear in the sermons on John whether integration into community is a part of redemption itself or whether it is a consequence of redemption. It is not clear from the separation of forgiveness from reintegration into community, which Schleiermacher highlighted in his reading of John 21, that Schleiermacher understood reintegration to be the final step in redemption.

In an essay on Resurrection and Ascension sermons, Emanuel Hirsch suggested that Schleiermacher interpreted the forty days between the Resurrection and Ascension as the foundation of Christian community. Hirsch referred to this period as the "second life" of Jesus and described Schleiermacher's position as presenting Christian community as the immediate work of Jesus of Nazareth in this period.[99] The Johannine sermons, which Hirsch does not discuss, suggest an alternative to Hirsch's description. In Schleiermacher's preaching on John, the Redeemer engaged in fostering community both prior to his death and in the period between the Resurrection and Ascension. The Resurrection appearances secure

97. Kurt Gerhard Jung, *Der Erlösungsbegriff,* 79 and 82.

98. SW II/1:154–69 (Acts 17:24–27 2.11.1800) "Die Gemeinschaft des Menschen mit Gott." (This sermon was edited and published by Schleiermacher in 1801 in the first Predigtsammlung.)

99. Hirsch, *Schleiermachers Christusglaube,* 59.

what has already been formed, just as the death and Ascension secure an understanding of the nature of faith that was formed through the earlier work of the Redeemer. Hirsch's description places too much weight upon a decisive change occurring at the Crucifixion and does not account for Schleiermacher's interpretation of the Redeemer's work prior to his death. In particular, Hirsch does not take into account Schleiermacher's description of persons who experienced redemption through their direct encounters with the Redeemer, and he ignores the active role Schleiermacher attributed to Jesus in bringing people into Christian community prior to the Crucifixion. Furthermore, if the Resurrection appearances were foundational for Christian community, as Hirsch suggests, we would expect these texts to be used throughout the year, or at least to be echoed in preaching in other seasons. Instead, we find that our records show only one instance in which the appearances in John were used outside Eastertide. Moreover, appearance texts are not often echoed in other preaching, unlike John 6:68 and 15:12, which are not appearance texts. The Resurrection appearances secure that Christian community that has already been formed around the Redeemer during his lifetime.

It is apparent to all who come into the sphere of Jesus' influence that he is the Redeemer. Redemption is available through the Redeemer prior to his death and Resurrection. Redemption is directly associated with incorporation into a community of Christians. These are the major presuppositions that formed an interpretive frame of reference for Schleiermacher's preaching on the Gospel of John. As is indicated by its absence from our discussion, Schleiermacher did not attempt to justify the truthfulness of any one of these presuppositions as he used them in his preaching. Demonstration of the coherence of the presuppositions in a reflective, systematic description of Christian faith is the task of dogmatics, not preaching, according to the organization of Schleiermacher's *Brief Outline*. It is to the dogmatics that we turn our attention in the next chapter.

4

A Reading of Christian Faith in Light of Schleiermacher's Preaching on the Gospel of John

> *. . . what I understand as pious feeling is not derived from a representation, but is the original expression of an immediate existential relationship.*[1]

WHAT particular kind of Christian relational experience might Schleiermacher have had in mind as he described pious feeling in the abstract manner demanded by the systematic format of *Christian Faith*? The answer to this question proposed in this chapter begins to illuminate both the structure of this exposition of doctrines of faith and the relationship between Schleiermacher's systematic thought and his practice of preaching.

This chapter identifies three strands of relationship between Schleiermacher's preaching on the Gospel of John and his dogmatic work *Christian Faith*.[2] The first strand is structural. I will argue that a particular kind of experience that may occur for preachers illuminates the presence of an underlying thought structure of *Christian Faith*. The second strand involves content. The content of the systematic exposition of *Christian Faith* provides a dogmatic context for the three ideas identified in the previous chapter as major presuppositions in Schleiermacher's preaching on John. The third strand is the use Schleiermacher made of Johannine texts and terminology in *Christian Faith*.

1. *Sendschreiben an Lücke*, 15; trans., Duke and Fiorenza, *Letters to Lücke*, 40.

2. *Der christliche Glaube* was published in two distinctly different editions. The first appeared in 1821/22 and has never been translated into English. The second and significantly rewritten edition appeared in 1830/31. The first English translation of the second edition appeared in 1928 and stands in need of replacement. A new translation by Tice, Kelsey, and Lawler is in preparation for publication by Westminster John Knox Press.

Strand One

The exposition developed in *Christian Faith* assumes that Christian piety is a fact and that we can talk about it intelligibly and analyze it critically. Schleiermacher distinguished dogmatics from apologetics, in part, by their different relationships to Christian piety. Dogmatics *presupposes* the fact of Christian piety and proceeds by interpreting it, presenting it in a rigorously systematic form that constitutes a whole. Thus, dogmatics clears up such misconceptions as tend to arise in the process of communicating the immediate Christian life.[3] It is directed toward those who live within the realm of Christian religious self-consciousness in a particular historical context. Apologetics, in contrast, is directed to those who think they find some decisive conflict between (objective) speculative consciousness and (subjective) religious (Christian) self-consciousness.[4] *Dogmatics* presupposes both Christian piety and therefore also God, toward whom that piety is directed. *Christian Faith* is a work of dogmatics.

The vocation of dogmatics is to clear up misconceptions that occur in the process of sharing an "immediate religious communication" of Christian piety. Dogmatics exists for the sake of clarity in this communication.[5] The means dogmatics uses for this purpose are comprised of skillfully defined and consistently used language. The German term for "communication," *Mitteilung*, is the same term Schleiermacher used for the vehicle of redemption in Christ.[6] Accordingly, the clarity provided by dogmatics is finally for the sake of sharing redemption itself.

Schleiermacher characterized the academic disciplines as either beginning from principles out of which the entire discipline develops (e.g. philosophy), or beginning with a particular range of external perceptions or observations (e.g. empirical sciences). In contrast to both of these, dogmatics begins by *postulating* the inner *fact* of Christian piety. In other words, dogmatics begins with something that is recognizably manifest in history but dogmatics works with it as a postulate, as something taken to be true in order to develop an account from it. In §27.4 this fact of Christian piety is discussed as an "*innere Erfahrung*"—an inner experience—"experience" having connotations of empirically as well as speculatively available knowledge viewed as practical knowledge.[7] Later in his exposition, this

3. *Der christliche Glaube* 2nd ed., §28.1 and §28.2
4. Ibid., §28.3, 1:160; trans., Mackintosh, 122.
5. Ibid., §28.1, 1:157; trans., Mackintosh, 119; the German text is clear on this point.
6. I will return to this point again later in the chapter.
7. *Der christliche Glaube* 2nd ed., §27.4, 1:154; trans., Mackintosh, 117.

inner experience is identified with Christian pious consciousness.[8] Thus, Christian piety and pious consciousness may be observed (though not in the sense of an empirical manner that stands by itself and is publicly verifiable) and analyzed.

What is made explicit in §88.3 is clearly assumed throughout: The communication of the absolutely powerful God-consciousness found in Christ can be and is *experienced* in Christian community.[9] Christian piety exists in such a way that it may be submitted to critical reflection, though it is not possible to prove in a speculative manner the necessity of the relations as they in fact appear. It is possible to deny the reality of how relations are found in fact. Schleiermacher's response to such denials further emphasized the importance of experience:

> These denials do not admit of being disproved; rather, they may be removed only through action in which we seek to cause those who deny to experience the same thing.[10]

Christian piety and Christian pious (or religious) consciousness as experience and therefore as facts for analysis are never far from any paragraph of *Christian Faith*. Misreadings of the text may easily result from any effort to ignore that close relationship between Christian piety and dogmatic exposition.

A Hypothesis

If Christian piety in the mode of inner and shared experience is always presupposed in *Christian Faith*, is there a particular form of such experience that illuminates the text? I suggest an hypothesis, namely: A particular kind of Christian experience offers a point of analogy between Christian piety and Christ's God-consciousness.

The particular experience referred to in the hypothesis is both individual and corporate. It is experienced by individuals in the presence of and in relation to both God and other persons. In grace-filled moments of preaching or of free prayer on behalf of those present, the speaker may become an open channel of that grace, active in its expression yet without attention to self as speaker and instead focused upon the message, its source, and those to whom it is directed. While the words are his or her own, they express more than the speaker knows to say. Upon later reflection, the ac-

8. Ibid., §64.1, 1:348; trans., Mackintosh, 265.

9. Ibid., §88.3, 2:21.

10. Ibid., §100.3, 2:93–94, my translation. The Mackintosh translation contains a misleading error in its reading of the German text.

tivity of that moment is often attributed to a divine source beyond the self but one operating through the self. In the moment, however, the speaker is so focused upon the communication itself that awareness of divine activity is peripheral. Part of the difficulty involved in describing the experience is that such description requires a highly nuanced language conceptualizing human consciousness.

The experience does not occur automatically in every act of prayer or preaching. The speaker may not will it to occur but may be more or less open to it on any given occasion. It is a corporate experience in that it does not occur when one is praying simply for oneself; it occurs in community, in a simultaneous relationship to other persons and to God.[11]

Indications of the Particular Experience in Schleiermacher's Writing

I begin to make my case for the illuminative power of such an experience in relation to Schleiermacher's dogmatic thought by pointing to indications of it in his early and late work. Readers of the 1799 edition of the *Speeches* might recognize a reflection of the experience both in Schleiermacher's description of religion and in his description of his compulsion to speak to them:

> Religion's essence is neither thinking nor acting but intuition and feeling. It wishes to intuit the universe, wishes devoutly to overhear the universe's own manifestations and actions, longs to be grasped [*ergreifen*] and filled by the universe's immediate influences in childlike passivity.[12]

This experience of being grasped and filled is not, however, generated by the recipient of it.

> All intuition proceeds from an influence of the intuited on the one who intuits, from an original and independent action of the

11. Hayo Gerdes described Schleiermacher as having an understanding of Christ in the heart directing a person of faith. But Gerdes did not attempt to reference a particular experience of piety. *Der geschichtliche biblische Jesus*, 103–4. D. Henri Roy argued that select sermons show that Schleiermacher both pointed to "divination" in his preaching and himself had a divinatory nature, by which Roy meant the capacity to discern and acknowledge the holy in its appearance. Roy did not attempt to describe an experience of divination. "Das unmittelbare Erleben," 115–23.

12. *Reden* 1st ed., 29; trans., Crouter, *Speeches* 1st ed, 102.

> former, which is then taken up [*aufgenommen*], apprehended, and conceived by the latter according to one's own nature.[13]

Thirty years later in the second edition of *Christian Faith*, Schleiermacher was still using the verbs *ergreifen* and *aufnehmen* to describe the action by the divine in relation to the human in Christ and the action of God in Christ in relation to persons of faith. What distinguishes the experience referred to in the hypothesis from these two familiar quotations is the mediating function in the experience; what is received and fills the recipient is received for the express purpose of both delighting in it and passing it on, sharing in it. It is indeed a personal experience but one that does not exist outside of a communal context.

The descriptive choices Schleiermacher made as he justified his address to his audience in the first speech reflect his sense that a larger power was at work through his efforts: a power to which he "submitted" himself and which "permeated" his being, a power that can be mediated.[14] Although his description of intuition in the *Speeches* is not always directly set in a communal context, as it is explicitly in the fourth discourse, his description of his own compulsion to "speak" specifically arises from an impulse to mediate a particular perception of reality and to awaken it in his readers. So, as early as 1799, well before Schleiermacher began lecturing on dogmatics, reflections of the experience I have described were already appearing in his writing about religious experience.

Such reflections of the experience were still visible at the other end of Schleiermacher's career. The fully developed dogmatics in the 1831 edition of *Christian Faith* reflects the experience that in its most central components accounts for redemption achieved in Christ. For instance:

> Since now the individual life of each proceeds in consciousness of sin and imperfection, we can find ourselves in the community of the Redeemer only insofar as we are not conscious of our individual lives; rather, as he gives us the impulse we find that that from which everything in him comes is also the source of our activity, a common possession so to speak.[15]

The absence of an ordinary, individualized consciousness of self, the impulse that comes from outside oneself, and the sense of common action

13. Ibid., 31; trans., Crouter, *Speeches* 1st ed., 104 modified slightly.
14. Ibid., 7–9; trans., Crouter, *Speeches* 1st ed., 81–87.
15. *Der christliche Glaube* 2nd ed., §100.1, 2:90, my translation.

are all characteristic of the hypothesized experience. Statements that touch upon this experience are more plentiful than space permits detailing.[16]

An Underlying Structure of Christian Faith

I argue that a closer examination of *Christian Faith* in light of the experience I have described will reveal an underlying structure of the work. Let us begin to test this claim by examining Schleiermacher's description of what is communicated through preaching. We turn to the exposition of §108 concerning conversion:

> [T]he self-revelation of Christ is now mediated by those who preach him; but they are being appropriated by Him as His instruments, the activity really proceeds from Him and is essentially His own.[17]

Redemption itself is communicated in preaching. Because the self-revelation of Christ can be mediated in such a way that it is his own self-revelation that occurs in the preaching of later persons of faith, Schleiermacher was able to argue that it is still the self-revelation of Christ himself that redeems. However, it is the quality of the experience itself to which I draw your attention. Those who preach are "appropriated" and their activity comes from beyond themselves, but their own activity is also implied in that they are preachers and neither mediums nor possessed—not even by the Spirit. The experience that I have described fits the parameters of Schleiermacher's more abstractly conceptualized description of preaching. Note, however, that Schleiermacher's concept of preaching is defined so as to attribute the divine agency found in the experience specifically to Christ.

I argue that Schleiermacher's description of sanctification may be read as a generalization of a Christologically modified version of the experience I have described. In the first edition of *Christian Faith* he described sanctification as resulting in all the activity of the person of faith becoming "a lively organ of the divine nature of Christ."[18] In the second edition §110 itself makes the operation of Christ through believers explicit:

> In living community with Christ the natural powers of the regenerate are appropriated for his use, whereby a life related to his

16. For example, I find direct reflections of the experience in more than 30 important passages in the second edition of *Christian Faith*.

17. Ibid., §108.5, 2:165; trans., Mackintosh, 491.

18. *Der christliche Glaube* 1821/22, §132.5, 2:148, my translation.

> perfection and blessedness is formed. This life is called the state of sanctification.[19]

I suggest that the kind of experience I have described is an example of such appropriation. Schleiermacher generalized the experience of being appropriated beyond preachers to all persons of faith and beyond the preaching moment to make it the defining condition of the sanctified or blessed life.

This picture of sanctification is intelligible only to the extent that it is consistent with the picture of redemption and its cause. By the explicit rules of Schleiermacher's dogmatic logic, the origination of a spiritual state and the continuation of it must derive from the same impulse.[20] Thus, since the state of sanctification is one of living communion with God in Christ, regeneration must be described as the origination of that living community.[21] Conversion constitutes Schleiermacher's account of regeneration viewed as a human experience, and justification constitutes his account of regeneration viewed as a divine activity.

Justification was understood by Schleiermacher to be a result of the single eternal divine decree—a decree which is expressed temporally in creation and preservation, justification and sanctification. From the temporal, human perspective conversion is caused by encounter with Christ, an encounter in which a particular pattern of relationship is established. Schleiermacher described this relationship between Christ and persons of faith as a parallel to the relationship between the divine and human within Christ himself. In formulaic terms: divine is to human within Christ as Christ is to persons of faith.

The parallel between Christ and ourselves is explicit and consistent both in Schleiermacher's description of the parallel itself and in his conceptualizations of the effectiveness of Christ and of the dignity of Christ. Now, §88 is part of the introduction to that subsection of *Christian Faith,* which focuses on describing the consciousness of grace:

19. *Der christliche Glaube* 2nd ed., §110, 2:182, my translation.

20. Ibid., §127.2, trans., Mackintosh, 587 ". . . spiritual states depend upon the mode of their origination." §97.1 also indicates that every moment of the state of union between the divine and the human in Christ is a new expression of the union, so that the beginning and the continuation of the union must exemplify the same state.

21. Schleiermacher's term is "*Lebensgemeinschaft.*" I prefer translating this to "living community" rather than the Mackintosh translation to "living fellowship" because *Gemeinschaft* and community have similar valences to commonality, communal, communion, and individual relationships occurring within the context of a larger body of persons. The German word also has close associations with Schleiermacher's term for a congregation—*Gemeine.*

> In this common life, which goes back to the effectiveness of Jesus, redemption is achieved by him by virtue of the communication [*Mitteilung*] of his sinless perfection.[22]

Note the central role of *Mitteilung* as the act which redeems. The verb form, *mitteilen*, was used to describe the *divine* activity in the union of the divine and human natures in Christ in §97:

> In the uniting of the divine nature with the human the divine alone was active or communicating itself [*sich mitteilend*], and the human alone was passive or receptive; during the union of the two, however, every activity was also one common [*gemeinschaftliche*] to both.[23]

The awkwardness of expression in this proposition results from Schleiermacher's apparent wish to remain faithful to the intentions of the Council of Chalcedon while engaging in a critique of Chalcedonian language. Note that the adjective used to describe the relationship between the natures in union is the same root as the noun, *Gemeinschaft*, which Schleiermacher consistently used to describe the relationship between persons of faith and God through the Redeemer and among persons of faith themselves. So, the key terms for describing the initiation and the continuation of union are the same in Schleiermacher's description both of the union of the human and divine in Christ and in his description of the redemptive relationship between Christ and those who have faith and even for the relationships among persons of faith.

The parallel is most frequently used in the second edition of *Christian Faith* to illuminate the relationship between Christ and persons of faith.[24] This practice is a function of the organization of the work, in which the doctrines of Christ's nature and work precede the doctrines of regeneration and sanctification. The way Schleiermacher knew the nature of Christ worked in the opposite direction: the nature of Christ is inferred from its effects through Schleiermacher's construction of Christ as ideal and through his understanding of the power of the presence of an ideal to evoke or create reflections of itself.[25] The parallel between Christ and ourselves is

22. *Der christliche Glaube* 2nd ed., §88, 2:18, my translation.

23. Ibid., §97, 2:58, my translation.

24. For examples of his use of the parallel see ibid, §101.2, 2:99; trans., Mackintosh, 433 and §105.1, 2:138; trans., Mackintosh, 468 and §106.1, 2:148; trans., Mackintosh, 477 and §108.6, 2:171; trans., Mackintosh, 495 and §109.4, 2:182; trans., Mackintosh, 503–504 and §110.3, 2:187; trans., Mackintosh, 509 and §112.1, 2:200; trans., Mackintosh, 519 and §112.2, 2:200; trans., Mackintosh, 519.

25. Ibid., §93.2, 2.35; trans., Mackintosh, 378.

interesting but not redeeming in itself unless one accepts Schleiermacher's construction of *Urbildlichkeit*—ideality which is inherently reproductive of itself.

Schleiermacher's claim for Christ's ideality is a limited claim: It does not include the thousands of different internal and external human relations; it focuses upon only one—"the capacity of the God-consciousness to give the impulse to all life's experiences and to determine them."[26] The difference between an example and the ideal is one of degree and influence. The ideal is an example, but unlike any other example, the ideal may never be surpassed either theoretically or in history. The ideal is unique. So, the content of the claim for the ideality of Christ is "that no more perfect form of God-consciousness lies before the human race."[27]

The ideal is further distinguished from the exemplary by its power to produce every possible improvement in the totality.[28] Schleiermacher did not clarify in §93 how an ideal produces. He assumed that his readers agreed both with his claim that Christ is productive (perhaps based upon their own experience) and with his claim about the unique ability of ideality to be productive. This ideality is productive; it may never be produced, because if it were produced Christ would be the first to be redeemed thereby and only afterwards be redeeming.[29] If one were to posit such a two-stage process, it would imply a more powerful agent's initiating the first step and then surpassing it. Being surpassed denies the ideality of that which is surpassed. In the same way, if an external criterion were used to distinguish the ideality seen in Christ from what is non-ideal, this criterion would be superior to the Redeemer himself. Since by definition nothing may be superior to a true ideality, every moment of Christ's ideal life must itself be defined by his ideality, and that ideality must be ideal in the same way for all individuals in spite of their differences.[30]

As Schleiermacher has constructed the ideality of Christ, if blessedness and perfection are the content of living community with Christ, then Christ himself must possess unbroken blessedness and perfection. Blessedness was related to human experience in Schleiermacher's interpretation of sanctification; blessedness is a benefit of assimilation to Christ and describes the condition of sanctification. I have already suggested that the interpretation of sanctification may be read as a generalization of the

26. Ibid.
27. Ibid., §93.2, 2:34; trans., Mackintosh, 377.
28. Ibid., §93.2, 2:36; trans., Mackintosh, 379.
29. Ibid., §93.4, 2:41; trans., Mackintosh, 383–84.
30. Ibid., §93.5, 2:42; trans., Mackintosh, 384–85.

experience which I have described. In such a reading, then, the described experience may be used as an experiential reference point for Schleiermacher's conceptualization of the human and divine nature of Christ. The union operates similarly to the activity of the preacher under the "common spirit" shared with the community of faith in the preaching moment.

As was noted earlier, consciousness is introduced into this development of the implications of the concrete experience as a general category by the nature of the experience itself. The close parallel Schleiermacher drew between Christ and persons of faith required that he develop a sophisticated description of human consciousness in order to distinguish Christ from all other persons while maintaining the intelligibility of the claim for continuity between Christ and the rest of humanity. This description is provided in the introductory propositions of *Christian Faith* and at the transitions beginning the two major parts of the work, where it fits most appropriately into the linear exposition of a systematic dogmatics. However, the necessity for a discussion of consciousness results only from his understanding of the doctrine of sanctification and of the doctrines of the work and person of Christ.

What I have done in this section is to describe an experience that is not uncommon in Christian worship and then to follow reflections and developments of it through *Christian Faith*. I began with Schleiermacher's description of preaching as an event in which Christ appropriates the activity of persons in order to use them as mediators in his self-revelation, which I suggested was an abstract way of describing the hypothesized experience. I then turned to sanctification and noted how this singular experience is reflected in blessedness as a generalization of it into a seamless web of moments constituting a life. This blessed or redeemed life was shown to be initiated by encounter with its ideal form in Christ. Christ as ideal was described as completely embodying blessedness. So, we have a picture of Christ as Redeemer that may be read as being an extrapolation from or an attempt to account for a particular Christian experience. Furthermore, I suggested that it is the nature of this experience that requires the nuanced but controversial description of consciousness found in *Christian Faith*.

This analysis suggests that the underlying Christological structure of *Christian Faith* is a development from two points: a particular kind of experience from which a normative concept of redemption and blessedness was developed and an understanding of causality, which Schleiermacher used to interpret how it is that Christ may be understood to be the source of both the experience and the redemption and blessedness associated with it.

I am not trying to suggest that the dogmatics was written or developed in the order just described. I am arguing that in addition to the logic of the dogmatic exposition, there is a logic underlying it, which becomes evident when one begins by considering the specific kind of experience to which the dogmatics points and in which Schleiermacher is very likely to have shared in his practice as a preacher.[31] This underlying logic is profoundly rooted in the practices of Christian faith communities; it both begins with and explicates a lived Christian faith.

Strand Two

There is a second strand of relationship between Schleiermacher's preaching and *Christian Faith*. It involves the content of Schleiermacher's preaching on the Gospel of John and the content of his dogmatic exposition of the work of Christ. In the previous chapter I identified three presuppositions which undergirded Schleiermacher's preached exposition of John: it was apparent to all who entered Jesus' sphere of influence that he was the Redeemer; redemption was available prior to Jesus' death and Resurrection; and redemption is directly associated with incorporation into community. While *Christian Faith* does not attempt to provide proof for these presuppositions, it does clarify them by creating a detailed systematic doctrinal context in which their content is central.

It Was Apparent that Jesus Was the Redeemer

The presupposition itself (it was apparent to all who entered Jesus' sphere of influence that he was the Redeemer) has implications for what initiates redemption. Something about Jesus himself, rather than a result of his activity, must have been the source of his redeeming influence. No single activity appears in the Gospel narratives that is associated with every encounter between Jesus and persons who came to have faith. If a specific activity was not the source of redemption, then something about Jesus himself must have been the source. A dogmatic clarification and contextualization of the presupposition must answer two questions: What is it about Jesus himself that is redemptive; and how does whatever that quality is get transferred from him to persons of faith?

31. I am not aware of an explicit description of Schleiermacher's own experience while preaching. His letters refer to the process of developing a sermon but not to his experience of their delivery. If the described experience were explicitly Schleiermacher's own, we would not expect his sermons to reflect directly upon themselves, because the experience is not self-referential. The sermons on Johannine texts do not refer to themselves.

The answer to the second question can be more succinctly put: Jesus' self-communication of his ideality itself made possible reception of it and entrance into community with him. As we have already seen, Schleiermacher's construction of Jesus' ideality in the exposition of §93 claims for that ideality the power to reproduce itself. Stated another way in §88.2, recognition of the sinless perfection of Christ was and is a work of that perfection itself.[32] Whether viewed as reproduction of Jesus' ideality or as recognition of his sinless perfection, according to Schleiermacher spiritual influence is possible only through self-presentation in word or deed. Consequently, in order to be redeemed, individuals must enter into the sphere of Christ's historical influence, where they become aware of his self-revelation.[33]

Schleiermacher answered the first question (what is it about Jesus that is redemptive?) with a single phrase: his sinless perfection. The phrase is the focal concept of the propositions that introduce the largest portion of *Christian Faith*, which is devoted to explication of the consciousness of grace. §88 states:

> In this common life, which is based upon the effectiveness of Jesus, redemption is caused by him through the communication of his sinless perfection.[34]

That Schleiermacher here meant redemption in the broader sense of redemption and sanctification is made clear in the exposition: redemption entails surety regarding Jesus' possession of a sinless perfection and regarding the continued communication of this perfection in the community founded by him; redemption also provides for the removal of misery and for growing in blessedness. Removal of the lack of blessedness (*Unseligkeit*) is the result of redemption, and growing in blessedness is the condition of sanctification.[35] The communication of sinless perfection has both beginning and sustaining functions, because every moment of sustained faith is also an initiation of faith in that moment.[36] The sinless perfection of Jesus is the basis of redemption—including sanctification.

The meaning of the phrase "sinless perfection" depends upon the definition of sin. In general terms, everything which arrests the free devel-

32. *Der christliche Glaube* 2nd ed., §88.2, 2:21; trans., Mackintosh, 363.

33. Ibid., §101.4, 2:104; trans., Mackintosh, 438 and §100.2, 2:92; trans., Mackintosh, 426–427.

34. Ibid., §88, 2:18, my translation.

35. Ibid., §88.2, 2:19; trans., Mackintosh, 362.

36. Ibid., §112.2, 2:201; trans., Mackintosh, 520.

opment of God-consciousness is sin.[37] More specifically, sin is "inability for that which is given and strived for in our God-consciousness."[38] What is strived for is that the impulse or motive for every aspect of a life comes from God-consciousness alone.[39] From this perspective, sin is "an impeding of the determinative power of the spirit, caused by independence of the sensory function."[40] In the sinless perfection of Jesus his sensory functions are not eliminated, but they are always directed by impulses that arise in his God-consciousness.

The relationship between Schleiermacher's description and the creedal terminology regarding Christ was established by the claim made in §94: ". . . the continuous power of his God-consciousness . . . was an actual existence [*ein eigentliches Sein*] of God in him."[41] The significant issues engaged in the relationship between Schleiermacher's description and creedal terminology were clarified in three propositions concerning the person of Christ (§96–98). In them Schleiermacher addressed terminology concerning: the union of human nature and the very being of God in Christ (§96); the divine activity and human passivity and activity in the union of the so-called "natures" (§97); and the meaning of the sinlessness and absolute perfection of Christ (§98). The details of the person of Christ need not concern us for the moment as we consider Schleiermacher's preaching presuppositions—all of which have to do with the experience of redemption—because he addressed Christ's function as Redeemer in relation to persons of faith in his description of the work of Christ.

Redemption Occurs Apart from Christ's Death and Resurrection

The intelligibility of the second presupposition (that everything necessary for redemption is available in Christ prior to his death and Resurrection) is developed in two different places in the second edition: in the discussion of the work of Christ, particularly in §101 and §104; and in the postscript to the discussion of the person of Christ in §99.

Two different reasons are given in the discussion of the work of Christ to explain why the suffering of Christ does not have a primary role in redemption. First, if the suffering *were* primary, then the disciples could not have been taken into living community with Christ prior to his death. The evidence against this conclusion was so obvious to Schleiermacher that he

37. Ibid., §66.1, 1:355; trans., Mackintosh, 271.
38. Ibid., §89.1, 2:23, my translation.
39. Ibid., §66.2, 1:356; trans., Mackintosh, 272.
40. Ibid., §66.2, 1:357; my translation.
41. Ibid., §94, 2:43, my translation.

did not even state it explicitly. Clearly, the disciples *did* experience living community with Christ during his lifetime.[42]

The second reason for not giving the suffering of Christ a primary role in redemption is that ascribing a unique role for Christ's death would mean that, in regard to his death, his life as a whole would no longer be an example for human life and consequently would cease to be an ideal.[43] This ideality is the concept that Schleiermacher used to explain how Christ is the causal agent of redemption. If Christ is in any aspect not the ideal, he cannot redeem. So, Schleiermacher's explanation of Jesus' death makes that death different from others only in that Jesus responded to it differently. It is not different in kind from the suffering that humans experience in general. The acceptance of suffering and death allowed the Redeemer to demonstrate a blessedness that was not disturbed by suffering or death. The full dimensions of blessedness, therefore, are indeed apparent in the passion. In this sense alone, that the passion reveals the full dimensions of blessedness, can the passion be said to be the culmination of Christ's ministry. Thus, the suffering of Christ is connected to his redeeming activity but does not constitute it.[44]

Schleiermacher then reinterpreted the concepts of vicarious satisfaction and participation in Christ's suffering as being consistent with this understanding of the relationship between suffering and redemption. This was done by means of his description of the relationship between sin and suffering. Evil is the consequence of or punishment for sin, but the sinner is not necessarily the one who suffers the evil. Anyone may be said to suffer punishment for others in suffering the evil that results from the sin of another. Thus, anyone may be said to take away the punishment (by intent or not) of another. Accordingly, Christ, living in communion with humanity, could suffer and have compassion as a consequence of human sin and in this sense take away the punishment. This fact, however, does not distinguish him from any other human. It is not a unique act.[45] Redemption, in contrast, is a unique act, and therefore it cannot be a result of vicarious satisfaction of the punishment of sin.

In §99, to which is affixed a postscript to the section on the person of Christ, Schleiermacher specifically addresses the roles in redemption of the Resurrection, Ascension, and Judgment. The proposition itself excludes these three events from properly belonging to the doctrine of the person

42. Ibid., §101.4, 2:102; trans., Mackintosh, 435–36.
43. Ibid., §104.4, 2:132; trans., Mackintosh, 462.
44. Ibid., §101.4, 2:103; trans., Mackintosh, 437.
45. Ibid., §104.4, 2:126; trans., Mackintosh, 457–58.

of Christ.[46] The reasons include the recognition that these events do not fit the criteria provided in the introduction for what may be properly considered doctrines, and that they do not fit with the description of redemption provided. Two criteria for "real" (or "proper") doctrines are provided in §29.3: ". . . nothing concerning Him can be set up as real [*eigentliche*] doctrine unless it is connected with His redeeming causality and can be traced to the original impression made by His existence."[47] More importantly, these three events do not connect directly with the description of redemption provided in the rest of Schleiermacher's doctrinal exposition.

> For if the redeeming efficacy of Christ depends upon the being of God in Him, and faith in Him is grounded upon the impression that such a being of God indwells Him, then it is impossible to prove any immediate connexion between these facts [Resurrection and Ascension] and that doctrine. The disciples recognized in Him the Son of God without having the faintest premonition of His Resurrection and Ascension, and we too may say the same of ourselves; moreover neither the spiritual presence which He promised nor all that He said about His enduring influence upon those who remained behind is mediated through either of these two facts.[48]

The fundamental judgment which Schleiermacher made was that the disciples recognized in Jesus the Son of God without anticipating the Resurrection.

Redemption Is Associated with Incorporation into Community

The third presupposition (that redemption is directly associated with incorporation into community) holds together two distinct experiences, that of the original disciples who experienced redemption in relation to Christ before his death and that of all Christians since then who experience redemption in relation to Christ as communicated by word or deed in the community of faith. In the latter group redemption occurs within the context of community and is inseparable from it, while among the original disciples their direct relationship to Christ then drew them together into community. The completion of this process of community formation was not possible so long as Christ was physically present. Since the formation of community was and is the goal of Christ's ministry, his physical

46. Ibid., §99, 2:82; trans., Mackintosh, 417.
47. Ibid., §29.3, 1:163; trans., Mackintosh, 125.
48. Ibid., §99.1, 2:82; trans., Mackintosh, 418.

departure from his disciples was necessary for the on-going success of his ministry.

The exposition of the Reign of God in *Christian Faith* provides a context in which the presupposition is clarified, particularly in the description of sanctification. The community itself consists of the sanctified elements of everyone who is taken into living community with Christ. Further, what makes living community with Christ possible is mediated through this same communal life. The sanctification of each person depends upon the effective influence of the whole upon each individual.[49] Sanctification is itself measured by the relation of a soul to the service of the new communal life into which it has entered.[50]

The fulfillment of the Reign of God, begun simultaneously with the preaching of Christ, and sanctification are one and the same experience, to which Schleiermacher appeals with two different terms: the "Reign of God" in his discussion of the work of Christ, and "sanctification" in his discussion of regeneration and sanctification. The Reign of God is what Christ proclaimed. The name for living in it is sanctification. In the Reign of God an individual's relationship to God and that individual's relationship to the community of persons of faith are inseparable.

> The meaning of this is that in this Reign of God (which, it is always understood, is not of this world) the establishment and maintenance of the community of each individual with God, and the maintenance and direction of the community of all believers with one another, are not separate achievements but the same; and further, that these activities and the free dominion of the Spirit in knowledge and doctrine do not spring from a different source but from the same.[51]

The absence of direct argument for this position is easier to understand if the reader has accepted my suggestion that the particular experience that Schleiermacher has generalized and made normative for sanctification is an experience of an individual within the context of a worshipping community. An argument is not necessary if one assumes that experience; a simple description is sufficient as a reminder of it.

49. Ibid., §106.2, 2:149; trans., Mackintosh, 477.

50. Ibid., §106.2, 2:150; trans., Mackintosh, 478.

51. Ibid., §102.2, 2:106–7; trans., Mackintosh, 440. I have substituted "community" for Mackintosh's use of "fellowship" to translate "*Gemeinschaft*" and "Reign" for Mackintosh's use of "Kingdom" to translate "*Reich*."

The Three Offices of Christ

Schleiermacher's description of the work of Christ was elaborated in three propositions defining the "offices" of Christ (§§102–5). The interpretation of each of these offices provided substantial context for one of the presuppositions. The prophetic office was interpreted as Christ's self-presentation. The high-priestly office was interpreted as Christ's union with persons of faith, uniting them with the Father through himself. The kingly office was interpreted as Christ's founding and sustaining of spiritual community. A brief examination of Schleiermacher's interpretation of each office will serve both to fill out and to summarize the picture of the second layer of relationship between Schleiermacher's preaching presuppositions and *Christian Faith.*

Those who entered Jesus' sphere of influence directly encountered his self-presentation. Schleiermacher's description of the prophetic office made clear that this encounter was neither accidental nor incidental. The prophetic office consists in teaching, prophesying and working miracles.[52] In Christ "the Reign of God itself, however, is properly the miracle accomplished by Christ . . ." and its fulfillment began with Christ's preaching, which was both teaching and prophecy.[53] Teaching also occurred in conversation whenever persons were present who wanted to be taught. The context of that teaching was Christ's self-presentation, and because that self-presentation challenges persons to become what they are not, it is also prophetic. The impulse that impelled the Hebrew prophets was the point of connection between them and the prophetic office of Christ.

> As it was incumbent upon the prophet to satisfy completely through his speech the impulse that had become for him a divine impulse, and to render the entire content of it; in the same way the self-determination of Christ to teach was the task to completely satisfy the powerful—which is to say at the same time also creative—God-consciousness as it formed in his spiritual organ, and to render it in his teaching in such a way that the assumption of human being into community would also be effected thereby. For no other measure of the result and consequently also of the perfection of the teaching can be applied here.[54]

In this description of the prophetic office the self-presentation of Christ in his teaching reveals precisely who he is in relation to God and to persons

52. Ibid., §103, 2:108; trans., Mackintosh, 441.
53. Ibid., §103.1, 2:108; trans., Mackintosh, 442.
54. Ibid., §103.2, 2:111, my translation.

of faith: He is the Redeemer. To those who came into his sphere of influence this must have been apparent, because it was what he presented to them. The preaching presupposition becomes the obvious conclusion in Schleiermacher's dogmatic description.

The relationship between the high priestly office and the presupposition that redemption was available prior to Christ's death and Resurrection is less obvious than the relation of the prophetic office to the first presupposition. The high-priestly office is representational, but representation was redefined by Schleiermacher. It is not a covering or obscuring of sin like a blanket so that God does not see it. Nor is it an absorption of our punishment, vicarious satisfaction. Rather, the representational role of Christ is like that of a mediator, in this case one who both establishes our communion with the "Father" and supports our prayer.[55] However, unlike a mediator, who remains separate from both parties in a mediation, Christ's high-priestly office involves union with persons of faith. In this union, Christ's will perfectly to fulfill the divine will becomes active in them, so that the impulse to execute the divine will perfectly is shared by them even when the impulse is manifested imperfectly.[56] This shared impulse, made manifest in the exercise of the person's will, is what Schleiermacher meant by Christ's assimilation of persons of faith to himself. It is redemption. The description of the high-priestly office both excludes atonement theories as explanations of redemption and defines redemption as union with Christ. Such union may occur before, during, or after the passion and Resurrection.

The kingly office of Christ explicitly links Christ to the formation and sustenance of Christian community. Schleiermacher used metaphorical language associated with kingship only in the explication of this office. Here alone is the assimilation to Christ referred to as submission to his lordship. The metaphor allowed Schleiermacher to fill out his description of redemption in such a way that it is always related to a community comprised of persons of faith. The object of the kingly power

> cannot be the individual as such, but only a societal entity [*Gemeinwesen*], and any individual only in so far as one belongs to [it]. Individuals, then, submit voluntarily to the lordship of Christ; but in so doing they at the same time enter a societal entity [*Gemeinwesen*] to which they did not previously belong. Accordingly, in attributing a kingly dignity to Christ we are *eo ipso* declaring ourselves definitely opposed to the contention that Christ

55. Ibid., §104.5, 2:134; trans., Mackintosh, 464.
56. Ibid., §104.3, 2;124; trans., Mackintosh, 455.

> did not intend to form an organic community [*Gemeinschaft*], but that the union [*Verein*] among persons of faith came into being or was formed later, without his injunction.[57]

The sphere of Christ's kingship is the inner life of persons individually and in their relation to each other.[58] Accordingly, it is not concerned with arrangements of things of this world, nor does it use means common to the world such as threat or enticement to achieve its ends. Christ's lordship is the "purely spiritual lordship of his God-consciousness."[59]

The kingly office fills out the necessity for Christian community in a different direction from that taken in other locations in *Christian Faith*, where community is deemed necessary for communication of faith. In the metaphor of kingship, community is most clearly described as a part of the ongoing relation to Christ. Community is not only the means for the communication of faith, it is the only context in which persons of faith continue in relationship to Christ.

It is not uncommon for interpreters of Schleiermacher's thought to use illustrations from his preaching as further examples of a point derived from his dogmatic work. My analysis of the relationship between the basic presuppositions underlying his preaching on Johannine texts and the exposition of *Christian Faith* suggests a more integral relation. What I find is that what was presupposed in his preaching lay at the center of Schleiermacher's dogmatic exposition of Christ in *Christian Faith*. Thus, the second layer also highlights a profound relationship between *Christian Faith* and the living practice of a Christian faith community.

Strand Three

In the third strand of relationship between Schleiermacher's preaching on John and his dogmatic use of it in *Christian Faith* I draw your attention to the way the text and terminology of John itself was used by Schleiermacher. There are two features of note: the way in which Johannine texts were used as examples, and the limited use of λόγος and multivalent uses of "*das Wort*"/"the word."[60]

57. Ibid., §105.1, 2:137; my translation.

58. Ibid., §105.1, 2:138; trans., Mackintosh, 467.

59. Ibid., §105.3, 2:144; trans., Mackintosh, 473.

60. Schleiermacher used λόγος in the Greek characters on the few occasions when it appears in *Christian Faith*. He seems to have used it to designate the concept of a pre-existent divine entity which when united with the human is the second person of the Trinity.

Johannine Examples

Schleiermacher's exposition of *Christian Faith* was in constant conversation with the Johannine text, sometimes to use it to support his thought, sometimes to disagree with the text and to reinterpret it. If this is all that it means to have a Johannine theology—to be in critical conversation with the text—Schleiermacher's dogmatics is decidedly Johannine.

A close reading of the first edition of *Christian Faith* reveals at least six different kinds of uses of or references to Johannine texts.[61] The first use was to refer to Johannine texts for descriptions of the disciples that Schleiermacher used to illustrate a point.[62] Schleiermacher seemed to prefer the Johannine picture of the disciples. The second use was to refer to texts on the basis of which Schleiermacher appeared to have developed the particular theological judgment being discussed. For example, Schleiermacher was dependent upon the discourses of Jesus found in John for his evidence that the inner life of Jesus was central to his role as Redeemer.[63] In a third use Schleiermacher adopted Johannine metaphors or descriptions of Christ to sum up a thought, using the Johannine material as if he, with the church, had made it his own.[64] A very infrequent fourth use was that of using a text entirely out of its original context as an indication and support for a point.[65] In a fifth use Schleiermacher interpreted other biblical texts in light of Johannine texts.[66] Finally, in a frequent sixth use Schleiermacher specifically reinterpreted Johannine texts that seemed to disagree with his present description of Christian doctrine.[67] It is particularly in this last use that Schleiermacher most gives evidence of being in conversation with the Johannine text, using reinterpretation as part of the dialogue. As is true of all his citations of the Gospels, Schleiermacher's direct references to Johannine texts appear concomitant to rather than formative of his account in *Christian Faith*, though the Johannine depiction of Jesus' influence through his conversations is presumed without being directly referenced.

61. I have elected to provide this reading of the first edition rather than of the second because the critical edition of the first edition is more thorough in certain respects and facilitates such a detailed reading. It appears to me after a less exhaustive examination of the second edition that the two editions make substantively the same uses of John.

62. For an example see *Der christliche Glaube* 1821/22, §21.1, 1:82.

63. For an example see ibid., §118.3, 2:47.

64. For an example see ibid., §126.1, 2:100.

65. For an example see ibid., §96.2, 1:305.

66. For an example see ibid., §125.5, 2:96.

67. For an example see ibid., §57.1, 1:161–64.

Johannine Terminology: λόγος and Word

If Schleiermacher had anticipated the theological importance that would later be placed by Karl Barth and others upon "the Word," he might have been even more precise and consistent in his use of it. Although the λόγος (word) figures prominently in the opening verses of the Gospel of John, λόγος as it comes from Greek philosophy is not a central interpretive concept in Schleiermacher's dogmatics.[68] He referred to "*Menschenwerdung*" (having become human), but this concept was not tied to a pre-existent λόγος. The phrase *Menschenwerdung* emphasizes the incarnation as completed act without speculating about what preceded the union. This causes difficulties in describing "the second person of the Trinity," difficulties that Schleiermacher expressly tried to avoid by developing the doctrine of Christ within his systematic presentation independently of traditional doctrines of the Trinity and then pulling it all together within a critical account of what can be said about the Triune God in the conclusion.[69]

It is helpful to notice the difference between Schleiermacher's infrequent use of λόγος and his frequent use of the German *das Wort* (word). He did not use the terms interchangeably in *Christian Faith*. Schleiermacher used λόγος a very few times to designate the divine being that joined with the human nature to be the person of Christ.[70] These uses appear to me to occur only when Schleiermacher was referring to beliefs or doctrines articulated by others. In contrast to the theology implied in these uses of λόγος, Schleiermacher argued, among other things, that Christ's human existence would have been destroyed if he had recollected a separate existence of the divine in himself prior to his having become human.[71] Even if the λόγος was that which united with the human, the united person could have no recollection of pre-existence. Schleiermacher used Johannine texts against each other in support of this conclusion.[72] The dogmatic importance of a pre-existent λόγος was further denied in Schleiermacher's claim that what pre-existed the incarnation is unconnected with redemption in history and therefore cannot properly belong

68. A comprehensive study of Schleiermacher's various uses of the concept "word" in his hermeneutics, dialectic, and psychology lectures in addition to *Christian Faith* and his preaching remains to be written. It lies beyond the scope of the present study, however.

69. *Der christliche Glaube* 2nd ed., §97.2, 2:60; trans., Mackintosh, 400.

70. Ibid., §13.2, 1:91; trans., Mackintosh, 65 and §97.2 footnote, 2:63–64; trans., Mackintosh, 402–3.

71. Ibid., §99 postscript, 2:87; trans., Mackintosh, 422.

72. Ibid., §99 postscript footnote, 2:87; trans., Mackintosh, 422.

to Christian piety.[73] It is extremely misleading to use the term λόγος in relation to Schleiermacher's Christology because many of the valences of the term were explicitly rejected by Schleiermacher and he himself avoided using it.

When Schleiermacher used the term "word" its reference was to language and to an understanding of thinking as dependent upon language.[74] The word of someone refers to the whole expression of self through language. So Schleiermacher used "the divine word"[75] (and not λόγος) explicitly to mean the outward activity of divine thought, a distinction that is only an apparent one since he takes divine thought and activity to be one.[76] The Son was created through this divine word as a part of God's single eternal divine decree.[77]

When Schleiermacher used "the word" in relation to Christ it often did not have an attendant adjective. In these uses "word" is frequently multivalent, including both actual spoken words and a power behind them. In the following example, which identifies the word with the prophetic activity of Christ, "word" moves in the direction of both spoken word and power:

> Now in the first disciples both [faith and conversion] were effected by the word in its widest sense, that is, by the whole prophetic activity of Christ. . . . The constant factor is above all the divine power of the word (understanding the expression to the same extent), in which conversion is effected and faith still arises. The difference is simply that the self-revelation of Christ is now mediated by those who preach him; but in their being appropriated by him as his instruments, the activity really proceeds from him and is essentially his own.[78]

"Word" here means the self-communication of Christ as a whole. What Christ communicates is his relationship to the divine, a relationship into which persons of faith are assimilated. That the prophetic activity of Christ

73. Ibid., §105.2, 2:139–40; trans., Mackintosh, 468–69.

74. Here I am indebted to Richard R. Niebuhr's elucidation of the role of language in Schleiermacher's thought in his teaching and in our conversations about Schleiermacher.

75. I am not capitalizing "word" because German does not allow a distinction between "word" and "Word" to be made through capitalization. Schleiermacher made distinctions only through adjectives (such as "divine word"). The English translation, which frequently capitalizes "*das Wort*," makes an interpretive choice which tends to obscure Schleiermacher's multivalent use of the term.

76. *Der christliche Glaube* 2nd ed., §55.1, 1:291; trans., Mackintosh, 221.

77. Ibid., §41.1, 1:201; trans., Mackintosh, 154.

78. Ibid., §108.5, 2:164–65; my translation.

consisted of communication through words in language was made explicitly clear somewhat later. "[T]he prophetic activity of Christ consists in His self-presentation and His invitation to enter the Reign of God . . . ." The ministry of the word, or preaching, is a continuation of this prophetic activity.[79]

Schleiermacher used "word" to stand for the efficacious power in redemption—communication of Christ's self. This use was intended to do four things: First, his use of the word connected to Christ current preaching as an instrument of Christ's own preached self-revelation. Second, the word as a medium required the actual existence of the Redeemer who spoke it; this preempted the possibility that the idea of the Redeemer could be redeeming apart from its actualization in a person.[80] Third, the communication of the word of Christ required that things attributed to the mystical Christ today be consistent with the "original" words of Christ recorded in scripture, providing a check upon what can be attributed to Christ. Fourth, the word required someone to proclaim it in the present and therefore required participation in Christian community.[81] Schleiermacher concluded that Christ himself could not have communicated his self-consciousness without the use of words.[82]

Conclusion

Preaching as a personal experience, the presuppositions of Schleiermacher's preaching, and language or word provide three significant strands in the dogmatic exposition of *Christian Faith*. An experience occurring in the act of preaching is a point of analogy for the incarnation.[83] The preaching presuppositions are interpreted dogmatically so as to provide a Chalcedonian reading of the Gospel of John, a reading in which the full humanity of Christ is intelligible. The redemptive power of the Chalcedonian claim for both the full divinity (present in Christ's God-consciousness) and the full humanity of Christ is underscored. Finally, the Johannine text and terminology are carefully used in order to emphasize the communication

79. *Der christliche Glaube* 2nd ed., §127.3, 2:283; trans., Mackintosh, 590.

80. This argument anticipates Feuerbach's use of ideal Christology and attempts to forestall it.

81. Ibid., 2:167–68; trans., Mackintosh, 490–2.

82. Ibid., §108.5, 2:166; trans., Mackintosh, 491.

83. This is contrary to Dawn DeVries's observation: "For it is the incarnation of the divine *Logos* that serves as Schleiermacher's primary metaphor for the act of preaching." *Jesus Christ in the Preaching*, 48.

of Christ's self-consciousness as the experience of Christian piety in redemption.

Biblical criticism brings an understanding of what is humanly possible to the texts and makes historical judgments on that basis. The experience described in this chapter appears to contribute heavily to Schleiermacher's understanding of human possibility, which suggests that his experience of preaching itself also might well have contributed to his interpretation of the biblical texts. The interpretation of biblical accounts of Jesus is the subject of the next chapter.

5

A Reading of the Life of Jesus Lectures: A Historian at Work

When Schleiermacher first offered his *Life of Jesus* lectures in 1819 nothing quite like them had occurred before.[1] A new genre began to take form. He described his purpose in his notes for the 1832 version of the lectures: to "discover the inner quality of his [Christ's] life development as a unity."[2] Schleiermacher had already applied his principles of hermeneutics to individual biblical texts in his frequent courses on various books of the Bible. What made the *Life of Jesus* lectures different was the integration of various biblical views of Jesus into one picture on the basis of historical criteria rather than in an effort to maintain the inerrancy of each detail in each Gospel account. The lectures presented a kind of biography of Jesus, which is to say they presented Schleiermacher's conclusions from his critical reading of the canonical and extra-canonical sources, even though he insisted that an accurate, fully developed biography of Jesus' life would be unattainable. Reference to sources was used to substantiate the interpretation rather than being the focus itself.

The task that Schleiermacher set for himself in the lectures was ambitious and complex. He described it and the issues associated with it in the opening seven lectures. A "life description" or biography is a history. As such, it is more than a chronicle, which is merely an account of the content of a string of events. A history represents a whole as more than the sum of its parts. The particular is always related to the unity of the whole and

1. Hase, *Geschichte Jesu*, 1; Schweitzer, *Quest of the Historical Jesus*, 62; Hirsch, *Geschichte der Theologie*, 5:34.

2. *Das Leben Jesu*, 1; ed., Verheyden, *Life of Jesus*, 3—(Schleiermacher). This text consists of a combination of Schleiermacher's own brief notes for each lecture and an edited synthesis of student notebooks. Each note will identify which source, either Schleiermacher's notes or student notes, is being used, because Schleiermacher's own notes are a more reliable expression of his thought, though sometimes a cryptically brief one.

the externally perceptible is always related to something internal.[3] Thus by Schleiermacher's definition, contemporary research that seeks to isolate the words of Jesus in the Gospels and in non-canonical texts is developing pieces of a chronicle rather than a history. A sense of the whole is required in order to grasp the parts fully. Consequently, the goal of a proper history is to understand a life in its unity. One has achieved this goal only when one can describe how that unity would have related to particular circumstances other than those which occurred. This means that one is able to describe that inner connection which is the unity between responses to external events. In other words, the goal of a biography as *history* is to achieve insight into human character.[4] Such insight depends upon being able to describe and interpret the external and internal development of the individual. When Schleiermacher referred to the "*Wesen*" of Christ it was meant to signify this unity of inner and outer features, manifest in external, investigatable events.

The *Life of Jesus* lectures were the fruit of Schleiermacher's work as an exegete. Schleiermacher's theory of reading texts, his *Hermeneutics*, is currently the subject of considerable discussion.[5] This chapter will not attempt to enter the theoretical discussion of Schleiermacher's hermeneutics. Instead, it will provide a description of one portion of his actual practice of interpretation.

Schleiermacher rejected the idea that Scripture requires a special hermeneutics distinct from general hermeneutical theory. Consequently, Schleiermacher's notes and student lecture notes on *Hermeneutics* do not specifically address the problem created by the Gospels for historians of the life of Jesus. The object of historical interest, Jesus, was not the author of the Gospels, but Schleiermacher argued that if the Gospels were entirely fabrications of their authors and never recorded anything accurate about Jesus' life, then historical investigation of his life would be impossible.[6] He found it unlikely that Christian faith could have flourished as it has if the Gospels are entirely unreliable. Thus, in Schleiermacher's view a historical reading of the Gospels must concern itself not only with authorial intent but also with what can be ascertained about Jesus himself.[7]

3. *Leben Jesu*, 1–7; ed., Verheyden, 3–8—(Schleiermacher and student).

4. Ibid., 8; ed., Verheyden, 9—(student).

5. *Hermeneutik,* 2nd ed., Kimmerle, ed.; trans. Duke and Forstman. Other editions are available in English, each differently organized. There is considerable disagreement with Kimmerle's dating and arrangement of the texts. Moreover, in Schleiermacher's various accounts hermeneutics is interdependently paired with criticism as well.

6. *Leben Jesu*, 84–85; ed., Verheyden, 80—(student).

7. This chapter will not attempt to argue the point, but the reader will note that the

This chapter provides a reading of the *Life of Jesus* lectures which shows Schleiermacher functioning as a critical historian. This reading agrees with most of the conclusions of Dietz Lange and Royce Clark and questions the prevailing readings of Schleiermacher's critics.[8] The chapter proceeds by examining the *Life of Jesus* lectures to show the historical-critical tools that Schleiermacher used and on what basis he determined that the Gospel of John was his most reliable historical source. The next sections describe both how Schleiermacher interpreted the Johannine text in contradiction to some of the text's major theological themes and what Schleiermacher's interpretation of Jesus has in common with the Johannine interpretation. The relationship between Schleiermacher's historical-critical criteria and his understanding of redemption is described and contrasted in general with that of his critics. Then the claims of Schleiermacher's early critics are analyzed to show that the basis of their disagreements lies in the assumptions with which they began their own historical research. Finally, the implicit relationships between Schleiermacher's preaching presuppositions and his historical-critical biblical exegesis are identified.

Historical-Critical Tools

A careful critically controlled reading of the *Life of Jesus* reveals a complex picture of Schleiermacher as a biblical historian. On a cursory or biased reading, it is easy to miss the significance of the difference in prevailing theological and social psychological assumptions between Schleiermacher and later readers and to attribute the differences in historical-critical interpretations that result from those assumptions to a lack of historical acumen on Schleiermacher's part. Schleiermacher worked in a period in which the principles for historical criticism were still being formulated. His own principles of hermeneutics and criticism, conceived as aspects of the art of interpretation, contributed in a major way to a historical-critical method for reading texts. Schleiermacher was interested in reading texts not only as artifacts that arouse interest in themselves but also as sources for historical information. Thus, he insisted that only eyewitness accounts of events are reliable historical sources.[9] His principles of hermeneutics, moreover, ask about the entire context of a speech act—its setting, occasion, and purpose. Few of the Gospel accounts provide all of this infor-

chapter presupposes that the hermeneutics developed and used by Schleiermacher leads one to a historical reading of texts, that is, a reading in which discovery of authorial intent and a text's meaning to readers/hearers in the original context are the goals.

8. Lange, *Historischer Jesus,* and Clark, "Fourth Gospel and Christology," 17–35.

9. *Leben Jesu*, 48–49; ed., Verheyden, 47—(student).

mation. John is more likely to specify an occasion, and that is part of the reason Schleiermacher preferred it as a historical source.[10]

Schleiermacher was particularly likely to ask historical-critical questions when the narrated events are difficult to interpret because there are no analogies to those events in contemporary experience. For instance, in regard to the Ascension of Jesus, Schleiermacher asked: "What idea of the event did those people have who originally participated in it?"[11] This is a historical question, though it assumes that some kind of event occurred that was difficult to describe, an assumption perhaps not shared by some later scholars. He provided another kind of historical-critical interpretation of two other difficult events: the temptation of Jesus and the rending of the curtain in the Temple upon Jesus' death. In each of these instances Schleiermacher read the Gospel texts as narratives that have used a linguistic figure as if it represented a factual event: a parable in the case of the temptation and a symbol in the case of the Temple curtain.[12] In the period since Schleiermacher historians have identified this kind of narrative transposition of figure or symbol into fact much more frequently than he did.

Schleiermacher's literary analysis of the Gospel texts contributed to several of his historical conclusions. Observation of the tendency for accounts of miracles to appear at transition points in the synoptic Gospels contributed to Schleiermacher's conclusion that those accounts were more likely to be a part of the literary structure of the Gospels than to be eyewitness descriptions of events as they occurred.[13] He found it improbable that Christ before his death made use of Hebrew Bible texts to demonstrate that he must rise from the dead and much more likely that such passages were based upon what Christ was reported to have said after his death and were then ascribed to Christ's teaching before his death. This principle was used by Schleiermacher only to suggest that post-Resurrection sayings were attributed to an earlier part of Jesus' ministry. This application thereby allowed the sayings to stand as authentic sayings of Christ. Since the Gospel of John does not portray the resurrected Christ making use of Hebrew Bible texts at all, this interpretation did not threaten the veracity of John as an accurate historical source.[14]

10. *Leben Jesu*, 255; ed., Verheyden, 238—(student).

11. *Leben Jesu*, 495; ed., Verheyden, 466—(student).

12. *Leben Jesu*, 157–158; ed., Verheyden, 148–9—(Schleiermacher) and 449; ed., Verheyden, 421—(student).

13. *Leben Jesu*, 205; ed., Verheyden, 192—(student).

14. *Leben Jesu*, 478–479; ed., Verheyden, 449—(student).

Several critical insights were used consistently by Schleiermacher in his interpretation of the Gospels.[15] First, the Gospels as sources for historical reconstruction of Jesus' life are fragmentary and biased. They are insufficient sources in themselves for a real biography of Jesus, in which his development would be a major theme. Even the Gospel of John, which "gives the impression of a coherent, comprehensive presentation of Jesus," is an insufficient source for a real biography of Jesus, not least because of the absence of material concerning his development as a child, adolescent, and young adult.[16] Second, no sources from opponents of Jesus have survived that might have provided a meaningful contrast with the Gospel pictures. Such sources, if they ever existed, would have brought some balance in the face of any bias in the Gospel sources. Third, a historical-critical account of Jesus must examine all the available sources concerning him, rather than limiting itself to canonical accounts. Fourth, there are irreconcilable differences between the synoptic Gospels and John. Schleiermacher did not attempt a synthesis of the Gospels; he was willing to make choices between specific accounts on the basis of historical probability.[17] Among other principles for determining such probability, Schleiermacher used both preference for a simpler account over a more complex one and preference for a reading that is contrary to what might otherwise be expected or assumed to be the case.[18] Fifth, Schleiermacher recognized that an oral tradition or traditions pre-date and lie behind the written Gospels, particularly behind the synoptic Gospels. A major part of his preference for John depended upon his judgment (on literary grounds) that John was written as one coherent narrative by an eyewitness, this in contrast to the synoptic Gospels, which he read as compilations of diverse oral accounts. Sixth, Schleiermacher formulated questions that we now classify as central to redaction and tendency criticism, in particular the question of what principles of organization each Gospel writer used in determining the ordering of events in the narrative.[19] Seventh, Schleiermacher recognized basic ideas identified with Christ's preaching—such as Resurrection and last judgment—as having roots in ideas having accepted meanings in the culture

15. I have begun with, but also greatly expanded upon, six insights identified by Clark in "Fourth Gospel and Christology," 22–23.

16. *Leben Jesu*, 44; ed., Verheyden, 43—(student).

17. On the other hand, he was not willing to allow the possibility that any one of the canonical accounts is intentionally or unintentionally *deceptive* in its description of events.

18. *Leben Jesu*, 151–2; ed., Verheyden, 143—(student) and 457; ed., Verheyden, 429—(student).

19. Ibid., 39–40; ed., Verheyden, 37–39—(student).

of the first century.[20] Schleiermacher still identified the appropriation of these ideas with Christ himself, but recognition of such appropriation is in itself a critical insight.

These insights and interpretations suggest that Schleiermacher actually was a fairly sophisticated biblical historian. What differentiates him from his critics are not historical-critical tools but rather the assumptions with which they began their research efforts. The fact that Schleiermacher spent more effort defending his valuation of the synoptic Gospels than defending his acceptance of John as an eyewitness indicates that during his lifetime he perceived the greater challenge to be to historical criticism in general rather than to his specific conclusions concerning John.

John as a Historical Source

Schleiermacher had clear historical-critical reasons for his preference for the Gospel of John as a historical source: Understanding particular events or occasions for teaching requires setting them in the context of place and time and audience; John provides these details more consistently than do the synoptic Gospels; the text of John is more clearly a single, relatively seamless narrative in contrast to the obvious way in which the teachings are gathered together in the Synoptics, in accordance with different principles in the different texts. Had Schleiermacher had access to other sources for the same events narrated in the Gospel of John, perhaps he would also have recognized the aggregate qualities in the Johannine account. In the absence of other sources (and in the absence of a close knowledge of Palestinian geography), however, the Johannine account can be read as an eyewitness report of events—which is what Schleiermacher read it to be, following the traditional attribution of the Gospel to the disciple John.

Schleiermacher acknowledged in his 1832 notes for the *Life of Jesus* lectures a "prevailing opinion" that the apostle John had added his own interpretation to the tradition in the process of recording it. Schleiermacher's response to this idea was an elaborate argument, and it is instructive to notice the basis on which it is made. The argument was not an appeal to faith, nor an appeal to authority, nor an appeal to experience. The argument was built upon what Schleiermacher understood to be accepted empirical facts: Johannine authorship of the text, John's relationship to John the Baptist prior to his encounter with Christ, and the contrast between the mystical concerns expressed in the Gospel text and the message of John the Baptist. Schleiermacher argued that someone who followed John the

20. Ibid., 253; ed., Verheyden, 236–37—(student).

Baptist would not have found mysticism appealing. Since the apostle John was at first a follower of John the Baptist, the apostle is not the likely source of mysticism found in the Gospel. If the mysticism cannot be attributed to the apostle John, then the most likely source is Christ himself.[21] This argument depends upon acceptance of apostolic authorship of the Gospel, but that was still a credible historical position. What is important to note is the kind of argument Schleiermacher provided; he constructed a picture consistent with accepted historical data from the first century.

The stylistic differences in Jesus' manner of teaching between the synoptic Gospels and John were explained by Schleiermacher as resulting from a conscious response to the limitations of oral traditions, which were the sources for the synoptic Gospels. Oral tradition conveyed those words of Jesus that could not easily be misunderstood and misrepresented in oral repetition of them. In contradiction, the discourses found in John were more easily misrepresented and so were intentionally excluded from the oral tradition of the time. Since the Johannine text appears to have been a written narrative without an oral pre-history, Schleiermacher hypothesized that the apostle John had been free to record the more complicated discourse form of Jesus' teaching directly into writing without fear of alterations occurring through misunderstanding during transmission.[22] Because he emphasized the pervasive influence of Hellenism rather than the distinctiveness of Judaism in the first century, it was credible to Schleiermacher that Jesus himself might have employed a Socratic, interactive form of teaching such as that found in the discourses in John.

Schleiermacher's preference for the Gospel of John as a historical source had historical-critical warrants that were entirely credible in his lifetime. The charge that Schleiermacher preferred John for theological reasons ignores those historical-critical warrants and then ignores the significant ways in which Schleiermacher's interpretation of John rejects some of the strongest theological themes in the Gospel.

Schleiermacher Read John against Itself

Flat claims that Schleiermacher was uncritical toward John and that he developed an essentially Johannine theology completely ignore the preponderance of evidence in the *Life of Jesus* lectures that Schleiermacher regularly interpreted John in contradiction to some of the text's strongest themes.

21. Ibid., 274–75; ed., Verheyden, 256–57—(Schleiermacher).
22. Ibid.

Whether or not the Gospel of John is interpreted through the lens of its prologue ("In the beginning was the Word . . ."), the text tends to emphasize the divinity of Christ as the Son of God, the one who is different from all other persons. Contrary to the criticism that Schleiermacher posited an ideal in history, Schleiermacher was explicitly concerned with countering what he termed "docetic" tendencies in Christian thought. Docetism in Schleiermacher's use of the term refers to "abolition of the true humanity of Christ."[23] This occurs whenever the divine properties do not abstain from action in a particular description of Christ. Considering divine properties to be active in Christ is not harmful to faith, but it makes a coherent conception of him as a human being impossible.[24] Thus, it is not acceptable for Christian doctrine. The divine in Christ must always be thought of "in human terms in a human setting."[25] Christ never distinguished between the human nature and the divine presence in himself but always spoke in terms of the unity of his being.[26]

Schleiermacher's reading of John played down both activities and words of Christ that are beyond the realm of human possibility. He always described a *human* life and never a divine life masquerading as human. This reading required addressing specific texts that counterindicate it, texts such as John 17:5, referring to the glory Jesus had with the Father before the foundation of the world. This high priestly prayer in chapter 17 suggests at several points that Jesus pre-existed creation. Schleiermacher read this chapter in such a way that talk of a pre-existent glory is actually an anticipation of the redemption to be manifest through the life of Christ in the unfolding of God's plan in time.[27] This does not mean, however, that Christ recollects this time before the world existed.

> It would interfere with all human treatment of the subject and Christ would be a completely [phantom-like] figure if we were to ascribe to him either the recollection of a consciousness of a pre-human state of being along with his consciousness of his state of being as a man, or a parallel awareness of his divinity and his humanity.[28]

23. Ibid., 14; ed., Verheyden, 15—(student).
24. Ibid., 29; ed., Verheyden, 29—(Schleiermacher).
25. Ibid., 86; ed., Verheyden, 81—(Schleiermacher).
26. Ibid., 287–88; ed., Verheyden, 269—(Schleiermacher).
27. Ibid., 286; ed., Verheyden, 268—(student).
28. Ibid., 288; ed., Verheyden, 269—(Schleiermacher). See also ibid., 359; ed., Verheyden, 335, and ibid., 281–82; ed., Verheyden, 213, and ibid., 102–3; ed., Verheyden, 96.

Schleiermacher did not directly exclude the possibility of pre-existence, but he denied the apparent consciousness of it exhibited in the prayer of John 17.

A related issue was the question of what Christ knew and did not know during his lifetime. This issue also required careful interpretation, since errors of judgment were understood to result from sin or moral deficiency, neither of which Schleiermacher would attribute to Jesus. However, if Christ knew what was not generally known in his day, this knowledge would have been omniscient—reflecting a "docetic" view of Christ; and if Christ simply pretended not to know what he, in fact, did know, this would have involved his knowingly accepting human error—also inconceivable.[29] So, Schleiermacher interpreted Christ's knowledge in the domain of his vocation as developing without error, but outside of his vocation Christ's knowledge was the same as that of his contemporaries. This is not the obvious reading of Johannine narratives such as the encounter with Nathanael, in which Jesus elicits initial faith through his apparently miraculous knowledge of Nathaniel before meeting him.[30] Schleiermacher's interpretation of Christ's knowledge attempted to walk a fine line between error or deficiency in Christ's knowledge and claims to have knowledge that is beyond human capacity. Christ's knowledge was complete in regard to what is essential (his vocation) and partial, as is all human knowledge, in regard to everything else. This interpretation was consistent with his interpretation of the miracle narratives as well.

The specific miracles that are called "signs" by the Johannine text are presented by the text as instances in which an action by Christ breaks both expectations and apparent laws of nature and thereby elicits faith in Christ. In contrast, Schleiermacher insisted that miracles are never sufficient in themselves as grounds for faith. He avoided rationalist explanations of how miracles might have occurred and preferred to leave miraculous events unexplained.[31] This was possible because they are not relevant to the eliciting of faith. Schleiermacher maintained an open stance toward what is possible within the realm of the laws of nature: Since we do not really understand nature completely, we do not know what is possible in nature and therefore cannot say with certainty that an event is impossible in nature and consequently must be miraculous.[32]

29. Ibid., 119; ed., Verheyden, 112—(student).

30. See John 1:47–49.

31. *Leben Jesu*, 244–45; ed., Verheyden, 227–28—(Schleiermacher).

32. Ibid., 22; ed., Verheyden, 22—(Schleiermacher).

The miracles do exhibit the authority of Jesus, an authority that has to do with his relation to God rather than with his own power.[33] This is the reason they are included in the Gospels: The miracles demonstrate the authority of Christ. Everything comprehensible about the miracles attributed to Christ is understandable as a consequence of his office as Redeemer, that is, his unique relationship to God.[34] What cannot be adequately understood through this approach was simply left incomprehensible. Schleiermacher assumed that Christ wanted his life to be predictable and comprehensible to others, because those qualities are necessary if his life is to function as an analogy for the lives of persons of faith.[35] Miracles, as they are usually conceived, interfere with that predictability and comprehensibility, in Schleiermacher's view.

Although the Passion and Resurrection narratives in John are not so large a proportion of the entire text as they are in Mark, the Johannine narratives of the Passion and Resurrection are a significant portion of the Gospel. They are central to Johannine theology. The account is framed by two mentions of Caiaphas in which he observes that it is better for one person to die than for the whole nation to be lost.[36] While this observation is not explicitly linked to forgiveness of sins in a full-fledged sacrificial atonement theory, it easily moves in that direction. The Johannine text suggests that the Passion and Resurrection are central to redemption.

In contrast, the Passion and Resurrection were *not* central to Schleiermacher's interpretation of Christ or to his interpretation of the Johannine text. The physical act of Resurrection itself is not described in any of the Gospels. Schleiermacher used this fact to conclude that the nature of the Resurrection is not significant for faith. In the *Life of Jesus* lectures the post-Resurrection appearances of Christ were treated as if they are a revival of human life in complete continuity with Jesus' life before the Passion; he called these appearances the "second life" of Christ.

Claiming that the Resurrection itself is not significant for faith did not preclude Schleiermacher from arguing that the death of Christ was necessary. He laid special emphasis upon two sayings from John (12:24 and 16:7): "Unless a grain of wheat falls into the earth and dies it remains alone; but if it dies, it bears much fruit." This first saying was interpreted in light of the second: Christ's death makes possible the gift of the Spirit, and it is the Spirit that makes possible a wide dissemination of Christ's

33. Here I agree with Lange, *Historischer Jesus*, 107–8.

34. *Leben Jesu*, 223; ed., Verheyden, 209—(Schleiermacher).

35. Ibid., 244–45; ed., Verheyden, 227–8—(Schleiermacher).

36. John 11:50–52 and John 18:14.

redemptive activity.[37] The death of Christ was a consequence of his life's work, and it was a condition of the fruitfulness of the gift of the Spirit. It was necessary as a consequence of the work of Christ and as a condition for the future; but, as these terms themselves suggest, it was a transitional rather than a definitive event. Redemption involves more than atonement; it is a consequence of the entire influence of Christ upon persons, an influence that itself purifies.[38]

The changes that occurred at Christ's death made possible the formation of community among followers of Christ. During his ministry Christ laid the groundwork for this community, but his presence among them stood in its way because his followers would then relate directly to him and not to one another. For this reason, it was necessary for Christ to leave or die in order for his mission to establish the community to be accomplished. Schleiermacher observed:

> Generally therefore the death [of Christ is] not [seen] as something special, but rather, as a result of his life's activity or as a condition of anticipated fruitfulness.[39]

It was not that Schleiermacher denied or ignored the Passion and Resurrection. Rather, they were viewed as integral to the entire life and ministry of Christ rather than as novel and decisive events.

What takes the place of the Passion and Resurrection in Schleiermacher's description of redemption is the mediation of life through the self-communication of Christ. He required no particular plan for his ministry, because his effective activity was the pure communication of himself, which occurred by means of living interaction with persons.[40] The operative power in Christ, his life itself, is a life-communicating power.[41] While Schleiermacher made frequent use of Johannine metaphors in articulating the relationships involved in the communication of redemption, his use of the metaphors de-emphasized important theological themes in the Johannine text.

After carefully reading Schleiermacher's interpretation of the Gospel of John, we simply have no warrant for saying that Schleiermacher appropriated Johannine theology.[42] There are, however, significant differences

37. *Leben Jesu*, 340; ed., Verheyden, 346—(Schleiermacher) and ibid., 318; ed., Verheyden, 323–24—(student).

38. Ibid., 347–48; ed., Verheyden, 325–6—(student).

39. Ibid., 341; my translation—(Schleiermacher).

40. Ibid., 130; ed., Verheyden, 123—(Schleiermacher).

41. Ibid., 293; ed., Verheyden, 275—(student).

42. For a succinct statement of the reading that Schleiermacher appropriated Johannine

between the historical interpretation Schleiermacher provided of the Gospel that undergirds his portrayal of Christ and portrayals of the historical Jesus today. These differences are clarified by examining the criteria used for isolating the historical Jesus.

Criteria for Isolating the Historical Jesus

Schleiermacher used the criterion of dissimilarity in his historical research, the same criterion that is the beginning point for historical Jesus research in the late twentieth century.[43] According to the criterion as Schleiermacher used it, only those ideas that cannot be derived from first century Jewish thought could rest their inclusion in the biblical texts on a claim that they came from Jesus himself. Furthermore, contemporary use of the criterion *also* distinguishes the ideas of the early church from those of Jesus.

Historical Jesus research today has largely come to focus upon identifying sayings that are likely to come from the earliest stratum of sources, but it is cautious about identifying that stratum with Jesus himself. Sometimes that same research attempts to characterize kinds of behavior that might have been typical activities contained in the earliest sources and perhaps characteristic of Jesus himself. The early church is deemed to have had a vested interest in identifying Jesus with its own theology and activity. Sayings and activities that were neither typical of first century Palestinian thought nor typical of the early church were the most likely, among the materials saved in the historical accounts, actually to come from Jesus. (In the most rigorous contemporary positions these materials are attributed only to the oldest available layer of sources and not to Jesus himself.) The picture drawn is a collage of small units of distinctive material associated with Jesus or the earliest communities of persons of faith. Schleiermacher used the criterion of dissimilarity in an effort to uncover a somewhat different kind of picture of Jesus. Schleiermacher was interested in identifying details only to the extent that they made it possible to uncover the character of Christ as a whole, his "*Wesen*" (nature).

The criterion of dissimilarity in both the contemporary and the Schleiermachean versions assumes that Jesus was distinctive in his teaching and activity. This assumption is closely related to Schleiermacher's preaching presupposition that it was apparent to all who entered his sphere of influence that Jesus was the Redeemer. Schleiermacher used the criterion

incarnational theology see Creed, *Divinity of Jesus Christ*, 32–34.

43. The classic statement of the criterion of dissimilarity is found in Perrin, *Rediscovering the Teaching of Jesus.*

of dissimilarity to distinguish Jesus from Judaism.[44] He did not use it to distinguish the historical Jesus from the early church. At that point he added a second criterion.

Alongside the criterion of dissimilarity Schleiermacher used what I shall call the *criterion of continuity*: There is continuity between the teachings of the historical Jesus and those of the early church in all matters pertaining to redemption. Aspects of the Gospel accounts that were not thematic in the preaching of the early church were clearly not essential for redemption (which was communicated especially through the preaching of the early church). It is not that non-essential accounts cannot be historical but that because they are non-essential they did not need to be integrated into the early church's preaching.

A striking example of the use of these criteria was Schleiermacher's treatment of the conception and birth of Jesus. Christ's special relationship to God did not derive from the prevailing first century expectations of the Messiah, in Schleiermacher's judgment. Furthermore, no one was recorded in the canonical birth narratives as saying anything that expressed the nature of the relationship as it later developed. So, Mary and Joseph could not have learned of the Christ's special nature and thus have taught Jesus about it as he grew.[45] Consequently, Schleiermacher concluded, what Christ said about his relationship to God must have come from his own consciousness and in definite contrast to his context.[46]

Schleiermacher then moved from the criterion of dissimilarity to make a historical and theological judgment based upon the criterion of continuity. He read the various Gospel accounts as individual sources from distinct early church communities and noted that if the birth of Jesus was essential to faith, an account of it would have appeared in all four Gospels. Since the account appears in only two Gospels, it is clearly not essential for faith.

The discontinuities between the preaching of the early church as recorded in Acts and the letters and the teaching of Jesus as recorded in the Gospels led Schleiermacher to conclude that the *content* of Jesus' teaching was less important than the effect of his personal existence upon those who followed him. Thus it was not Jesus' words alone that were taken to be redemptive; it was his person and his mission as communicated especially through his words. On the other hand, the apostles did not add anything to what they had received from Christ. Differences between the

44. For an example, see *Leben Jesu*, 97; ed., Verheyden, 90–91.

45. Ibid., 95; ed., Verheyden, 89—(student).

46. Ibid., 97; ed., Verheyden, 90–91—(student).

early church and Christ were a result of differences in presentation rather than content. There is always continuity of content; it is Christ himself and his relation to God.

On the basis of the criterion of continuity, Schleiermacher explicitly rejected a distinction between the preaching *of* Christ and the early church's preaching *about* Christ.

> It follows that we cannot make a distinction between the teaching of Christ and the teaching about Christ. Rather, the teaching about Christ was central to all his teaching. To be sure, the Gospel of John contains more discourses in which Christ speaks of himself than do the other Gospels, but we cannot say that the others lack this element.[47]

Schleiermacher's own notes for the *Life of Jesus* lectures repeatedly interpret Christ's teaching or preaching through the synoptic Gospels' image of the Reign of God, an image whose living referent is Christ:

> From this we see how little truth there is in the distinction often made between the teaching of Christ and the teaching about Christ. Whoever wishes to regard the latter as something that belongs to the time after Christ must not only question John's Gospel but also the others, for everything that has to do with the [reign] of God is also a teaching about Christ.[48]

The theology of the apostles of the early church, when it elaborates upon the teachings of Christ, was read by Schleiermacher to be nothing more than a connected exposition of the fragmentary material from Christ found in the Gospels.[49]

What made this criterion of continuity credible to Schleiermacher was his theological understanding of redemption. If redemption was available to the disciples and others during the lifetime of Jesus (which he believed it was), it is reasonable to expect that there is continuity between that teaching and activity of Jesus himself which communicated redemption and the preaching and activity of the early church after the Resurrection, which also communicated redemption.

This theological understanding of redemption is a major point of difference between Schleiermacher and his critics. If redemption is a direct result of the death and Resurrection of Christ, then it could *not* be avail-

47. Ibid., 251; ed., Verheyden, 234—(student).

48. Ibid., 245; ed., Verheyden, 229—(Schleiermacher). See also Ibid., 259; ed., Verheyden, 243—(Schleiermacher).

49. Ibid., 299; ed., Verheyden, 280—(student).

able in the same way prior to his death as it was after his Resurrection. This is Schleiermacher's criticism of a theology of the cross. Associating redemption with the Passion and Resurrection requires discontinuity at that crucial event. Thus, the teaching and activity of Jesus, targeted to his audience prior to the redemptive act, must be expected to be different from the preaching of the early church about Christ; otherwise redemption does not involve any meaningful change. From the perspective of this understanding of redemption, the criterion of dissimilarity makes sense (differentiating the historical Jesus from both Judaism *and* the preaching of the early church), and a criterion of continuity between the historical Jesus and the preaching of the early church makes no apparent sense at all.

Both the criterion of dissimilarity and the criterion of continuity are historical-critical criteria. The decision about whether or not to use the criterion of continuity is a judgment about historical method, a decision that is influenced by the theological perspective brought to the historical question. It is a choice made in some theological context. When Schleiermacher is characterized as being "no historian," the immediate question is: To which variety of historical method does the statement refer and in which theological context?[50]

The Extent of Schleiermacher's Dependence on John

Dietz Lange stated flatly that Schleiermacher was entirely uncritical toward the Gospel of John, in contrast to his historical-critical reading of the synoptic Gospels.[51] This is an unfair characterization. Schleiermacher applied the same critical tools to all four Gospels. While he relied upon John as his best historical source, he clearly identified an authorial selectivity at work in the text that makes it a less than perfect historical source and no more satisfactory as a life or biography of Jesus than are the synoptic Gospels.[52] This selectivity or "tendency" in John has two aspects: a stress on the teaching of Christ, and an emphasis upon "the development of

50. Thus, Hayo Gerdes is typical of even sympathetic contemporary readers of Schleiermacher who typify him as "no historian" because Schleiermacher had a differing valuation of John and what Gerdes calls "indifference" to source criticism. The root of the judgments which Gerdes characterizes in this way is the criterion of continuity—which Gerdes neither accepts nor recognizes to be at work. See Gerdes, *Der geschichtliche biblische Jesus,* 31. Gerdes moderated this position in a more recent article "Anmerkungen zur Christologie," 112–25.

51. Lange, *Historischer Jesus*, 91.

52. *Leben Jesu*, 168–69; ed., Verheyden, 159—(student).

Christ's relationship to the people in order to make the catastrophe of his fate understandable."[53]

So far as we know up to this point (not having a transcription of his exegetical lectures in print), Schleiermacher did not, however, use the critical tools that soon were used to call the priority of John into question. For instance, he did not read the Gospel texts for allusions to events or controversies that occurred after Jesus' death. Neither did he use knowledge of geography to question the coherence of Gospel accounts. Since he had an explanation for the coherence of the Johannine narrative and for the difference between the discourses of John and sayings in the synoptic Gospels, it is the absence of some critical tools which were only beginning to be developed that allowed him to accept the Johannine narrative as his most reliable historical source.

So, how *is* Schleiermacher's interpretation of Christ Johannine? In two ways: First, Schleiermacher followed the Johannine ordering of events and adjudicated disagreements between the Gospel accounts by giving more weight to the Johannine account. As we have seen, this was based upon a historical-critical judgment that values John as a more reliable historical source than the synoptic Gospels.

Second, Schleiermacher portrayed Jesus as the one who communicates redemption through his person. In John this is a revelation of divine glory (John 1:14b) made evident in Christ's teaching, miraculous signs, Passion, and Resurrection. In Schleiermacher's reading of John, what is communicated by Christ is a certain way of being human in relation to the divine that is transformative of ordinary human experience. It is evident in the personal life of Christ *as a whole,* rather than in individual events.

The long discourses of Jesus provided in the Gospel of John suggest that the teaching of Jesus provides the key to redemption. Schleiermacher himself identified an emphasis on the teaching of Christ as one of the tendencies of the Johannine text.[54] However, Schleiermacher insisted that it is encounter with the *Wesen* of Christ that is essential for the communication of redemption and not particular teachings or even the teaching as a whole. The discourses were important in Schleiermacher's interpretation, because they repeatedly present occasions in which persons encounter Christ, develop a relationship with him, and come to grasp and be grasped by his *Wesen.* This understanding of the discourses as encounters rather than as teachings distinguished Schleiermacher's reading of the discourses in John from his reading of the sayings and parables in the synoptic Gospels. The

53. Ibid., 202; ed., Verheyden, 190—(student).

54. *Leben Jesu,* 202; ed., Verheyden, 190—(student).

emphasis in both the Johannine text and in Schleiermacher's reading of it is upon what Jesus says about himself. The discourses are a form of direct and intentional self-communication that makes possible the communication of redemption.

Schleiermacher's Critics

Criticism of Schleiermacher's historical reading of the Gospels began immediately. The most widely read critiques during and immediately after his life were by Ferdinand Christian Baur and his student David Friedrich Strauss. Baur's critique was based on his reading of the only published work of Schleiermacher's biblical criticism (a redactive-critical monograph on Luke[55]) and on his reading of *Christian Faith*. Strauss had heard some of the last series of *Life of Jesus* lectures during his stay in Berlin. The lectures themselves remained unpublished in any form until 30 years after Schleiermacher's death. By the time the lectures were published, the Baur reading was entrenched: Schleiermacher had superimposed his faith picture of Christ back onto the historical Jesus. On the basis of this reading, it was obvious that Schleiermacher was not an historian. Over the next century this uninformed and strongly biased view of Schleiermacher as biblical critic was repeated and amplified by Albert Schweitzer, and then by both Rudolf Bultmann and his followers and by neo-orthodox theologians.

Baur's objections to Schleiermacher's historical reconstruction focus upon the relationship between the ideal and the historical. The principal problem in Baur's view is that the Christian experience which grounds Schleiermacher's whole system cannot be traced to an effective cause in the form of a specific person who lived in history.[56] His accusation is finally that Schleiermacher's use of the idea of humanity pushes the historical Christ into the background as non-essential.[57] Baur read Schleiermacher to imply that for him the essence of Christ is something more than simply the appearance of Jesus in history, something that cannot be known simply in his appearance. This essence is formed by thought and fantasy and raises the Christ of faith above what is historical. Faith's picture of Christ is then read back onto the historical facts.

Some of the force of Baur's charge against Schleiermacher is a result of a difference in the assumptions each holds concerning the ground of

55. *Ueber die Schriften des Lukas*; trans., Thirlwall, *Luke: A Critical Study.*

56. Baur, *Die christliche Lehre,* 863.

57. Baur, *Die christliche Lehre*, 871.

faith.[58] Baur's position assumes that historical events surrounding Jesus, properly investigated, provide a necessary and sufficient foundation for Christian faith. Schleiermacher, in contrast, assumed that contemporary Christian piety is also a fact. He did not attempt to justify that piety upon a historical foundation, he took it as an accurate datum indicating a reality in itself. Christian piety is real and cannot be taken as a mere invention. Therefore, it must have a historical cause. So, when Baur charged that Schleiermacher had not demonstrated, but had instead presumed, that a relationship exists between subjective individual human consciousness and objective historical events, he was correct but had missed the point. For Schleiermacher, the Christological task was not to justify faith in Christ but rather to describe an existing reality, one that has a subjective side in the modification of pious self-consciousness and an objective side in the historical person Jesus who is the Christ. In other words, the boundaries of the task are created by empirically investigatable events, on the one hand, and statements of religious experience, on the other.[59] The reason one engages in historical research on Jesus, then, is to provide a clear empirical boundary for further dogmatic reflection.

Schleiermacher was quite clear about the nature of the religious interest that fueled his historical research on Jesus. "In the present state of the Christian church we cannot be satisfied to take our departure only from faith in him, or only from faith in the Gospel accounts as inspired truth. On the contrary, in this dispute our faith can become firm and direct only if we establish the facts quite impartially."[60] Schleiermacher's argument for Jesus' uniqueness was explicitly not an argument from piety. Rather, he asked whether the whole importance and influence of Christianity across history is adequately explained by the appearance of an ordinary person. In Schleiermacher's view an ordinary person obviously could not have had such influence.[61] This is a historical judgment.

David Friedrich Strauss challenged Schleiermacher more directly as an historian. In his response to Schleiermacher's *Life of Jesus,* Strauss' challenge was presented as a critique of Schleiermacher's readings of particular biblical texts. A significant theme of this critique was Schleiermacher's and Strauss' differing valuations of the Gospel of John as a historical source

58. Gerdes, "Anmerkungen zur Christologie," 112–125.

59. In this description of Schleiermacher I am following the argument made by Lange, *Historischer Jesus,* 81–83. For examples of Schleiermacher's use of the fact of piety as a boundary for thought see: *Leben Jesu,* 105; ed., Verheyden, 99 and ibid., 118; ed., Verheyden, 111 and ibid., 129; ed., Verheyden, 122.

60. *Leben Jesu,* 15; ed., Verheyden, 15—(Schleiermacher).

61. Ibid., 29; ed., Verheyden, 29—(student).

for data concerning Jesus' life and teaching. Since Strauss' first work was published the year following Schleiermacher's death, Schleiermacher never had the opportunity to respond to the challenge.

Strauss' overall, more Hegelian critique of Schleiermacher hinged on one claim by Strauss: The ideal, by definition, cannot exist within history, it may only appear at the end of a progression. Strauss argued that Schleiermacher was not historical, because Schleiermacher attributed ideality to a historical individual, Jesus.[62] What Strauss did not acknowledge is that his critique was based not upon the application of historical criteria but, rather, upon his definition of ideality, which differed from Schleiermacher's.[63] Schleiermacher was explicit that the ideal appears in history only in a form that can be humanly appropriated. This means that Christ is available to historical research. At the same time, Schleiermacher held that Christ himself provides the conditions for apprehending him. These are the parameters of Schleiermacher's basic assumption that historical research and Christian faith as expressed in pious self-consciousness are the boundaries of the field of investigation. Strauss, in contrast, was not explicit about the assumptions that underlie his historical method.

Albert Schweitzer provided the critique of Schleiermacher as an historian with some of its most enduring phrases:

> Nowhere, indeed, is it so clear that the great dialectician [Schleiermacher] had not really a historical mind than precisely in his treatment of the history of Jesus. . . . Schleiermacher is not in search of the historical Jesus, but of the Jesus Christ of his own system of theology; . . . Schleiermacher's dialectic is not a dialectic which generates reality, like that of Hegel, of which Strauss availed himself, but merely a dialectic of exposition.[64]

Again, the difference between Schleiermacher and Schweitzer hinges not on historical criteria but on the underlying definition of what constitutes "reality." Since Schleiermacher's historical interpretation did not agree with Schweitzer's prior definition of what is possible in "reality," Schleiermacher's historical interpretation had failed. Schweitzer tried to win his case against Schleiermacher on his assumptions alone, without even defining the "reality" that he judged Schleiermacher had failed to generate.

The fact that Schleiermacher developed and used historical-critical criteria does not mean that he used them completely consistently, or

62. Strauss, *Life of Jesus,* 885–87.

63. See Keck, "Introduction" in Strauss, *Christ of Faith,* l–lxxxii for a careful description of the changes in Strauss's position over his career.

64. Schweitzer, *Quest of the Historical Jesus,* 62.

that 175 years later we must be persuaded by his conclusions. However, disagreement with some of his conclusions is a far cry from dismissing Schleiermacher as being unhistorical.

In response to challenges to his biblical interpretation, Schleiermacher spent more effort defending his critical reading of the synoptic Gospels as historical sources than he spent addressing the few challenges to reliance upon John as a historical source. He perceived the greater threat to come from those who resisted historical-critical readings of the biblical texts. Changes in scholarly consensus in the 30 years between his death and the publication of the *Life of Jesus* lectures shifted the critical focus of his readers. Readers of the published lectures no longer assumed with him that an apostolic witness is a reliable historical source for the life of Jesus.

This change in assumption, if accepted, makes the historical task significantly more complex beyond Schleiermacher's execution of it. The increased complexity of the historical task distances us sufficiently from the life of Jesus that we find it difficult to attribute motivation or other internal thought processes to him. This sense yields a major difference between Schleiermacher and historians who immediately followed him. It was still possible for Schleiermacher to use a historical picture of Jesus as an exemplar for daily Christian practice. Since he could describe the mind of Christ, he could also project how that mind would respond in contemporary circumstances. This possibility allowed Schleiermacher to explain how encounter with Christ is still redemptive under very different historical circumstances. At the same time, his hermeneutical principles demanded that interpretation, if there is to be any, should rest on the results of historical-critical research. His effort in studying the Gospels, particularly John, attended to seeing whether there exists some continuity between Jesus, the early Christian community and later Christians in matters of faith and life, and he did find what he took to be strong warrant for indicating respects in which there is continuity.

Preaching Presuppositions and Historical Criticism

I conclude this description of Schleiermacher's historical-critical reading of John in the *Life of Jesus* lectures by making more explicit the relationship between his preaching presuppositions as identified in chapter three and his historical exegesis. I argue that Schleiermacher did not superimpose his presuppositions upon the biblical text but, rather, that the preaching presuppositions provided a context in which certain historical-critical criteria are more credible than others. Thus, the preaching presuppositions did not predetermine historical-critical judgments, but they did influence the selection of the criteria which underlie those judgments.

The preaching presupposition according to which it is apparent to all who come into the sphere of Jesus' influence that he is the Redeemer provided a context that makes the historical criterion of dissimilarity credible. It is the distinctive relationship between Jesus and what was traditionally presented as the first person of the Trinity, expressed by Schleiermacher in terms of Christ's consciousness of God, that defines the office of the Redeemer. This distinctiveness, tempered by the assertion that it is manifest in a fully human being, lends credence to a historical-critical criterion of dissimilarity.

The preaching presupposition concerning redemption's availability during Jesus' lifetime provided a context that makes the historical criterion of continuity credible. If the redemption experienced in response to the preaching of the early church and if the redemption experienced in direct response to Jesus during his lifetime are one and the same redemption, then there must be continuity between the preaching of the early church about Jesus and Jesus himself. The preaching about Christ must be an extension of the preaching of Christ. It must also contain a degree of adequacy necessary to provide such continuity, despite any flaws or conflicts.

The third preaching presupposition did not provide a context for a historical-critical criterion, but it did provide a context for one of Schleiermacher's significant historical judgments. The preaching presupposition according to which redemption is directly associated with incorporation into community provided a context in which association of the synoptic Reign of God teachings with a reading of the Johannine portrayal of the person and mission of Christ was credible. Schleiermacher's attention to the synoptic Gospels' emphasis upon Reign of God teachings was an important contribution to biblical research. He recognized the Reign of God as a means of describing possible but unrealized relations between persons in community. The Reign of God does not appear as a theme in the Gospel of John. The preaching presupposition that associates redemption directly with incorporation into community provided a bridge between a Johannine emphasis upon redemption as a function of the being of Christ and the synoptic Gospels' emphasis upon redemption becoming manifest in transformed human relationships. Thus, the third preaching presupposition created a context in which an integration of the two different biblical portrayals of Jesus' preaching was historically plausible. In contrast, a theological context in which redemption is understood to be a direct result of the Passion and Resurrection would lead one to a different emphasis. In this contrasting theological context, the difference between the synoptic Gospels' Reign of God teaching and the Johannine teaching supports the conclusions that the synoptic Gospels' account preserves material from before the Passion, and that the Johannine teaching is a theological statement from after the Resurrection.

Schleiermacher's preaching presuppositions provided a context in which the selection of certain historical-critical criteria and particular historical conclusions made sense. If readers of Schleiermacher do not share all of his criteria or his conclusions but do share his concern for historical-critical readings of Christian origins, part of the difference probably arises out of theological contexts that do not share his theological presuppositions.

6
Conclusion

In his preaching, dogmatics, and biblical criticism, Schleiermacher drew for us a picture of Christ, a picture of a human being who was acutely aware of that relationship to God that the rest of us know only dimly and experience fragmentarily. It is a picture that intends to return us to those moments when all that is within us is focused upon expressing that which yearns to be articulated in the community of faith: that which is healing, that which is perspective-making, that which empowers and accepts responsibility, that which gives life in the face of death. In those moments of focus we are most ourselves and are most able to be vehicles for more. We experience the possibilities of those moments in assimilation to Christ. This occurs not in passive contemplation of him as "other" but in an active re-presentation of his way of being fully human in relation to God. In Schleiermacher's picture of Christ, the divine is related to the human within Christ in the same way that Christ is related to those who assimilate to him. So, our representations of the relationship of the divine to the human illumine and enlarge our perception of the relationship between Christ and ourselves, and our experience of the actual relationship between ourselves and Christ illumines and enlarges our perception of the relationship between the divine and the human in Christ.

This picture of Christ has emerged out of an examination of Schleiermacher's work with the Gospel of John as a preacher, theologian, and biblical critic. In bringing this study to its close I draw your attention to some conclusions concerning Schleiermacher's thought itself, and I offer some preliminary reflections in the form of questions concerning his theological method as a model for other theologians.

I begin by recapitulating the progression of the argument. In the introductory chapter I described the relationship between disciplines Schleiermacher provided in his *Brief Outline*. I argued in chapter two that the variety of contexts for Schleiermacher's preaching makes it difficult to draw general theological conclusions from specific sermons. The third chapter showed that three presuppositions that undergird his preaching are consistent across his lifetime and across context and are even consistent when interpretation of specific texts changed. These presuppositions are: that everyone who came into the sphere of Jesus' influence recognized him as the Redeemer; that redemption was available prior to Jesus' death and Resurrection; and that redemption is directly associated with incorporation into community. The fourth chapter showed how Schleiermacher's *Christian Faith* provides a theoretical theological context for these presuppositions and suggested that the experience of preaching itself illuminates the structure of the dogmatics.[1] The fifth chapter showed how the preaching presuppositions provide a context in which two historical-critical criteria are made credible: a criterion of dissimilarity and a criterion of continuity. It argued that Schleiermacher used these criteria to portray Christ in contradiction to some of the main theological themes of the Johannine text.

Is Schleiermacher's Christology Johannine?

I am now in a position to provide an interpretation of the common assessment that Schleiermacher's Christology is Johannine. It is certainly the case that Schleiermacher used the Johannine account of the life of Christ somewhat more frequently than he used Matthew and Luke in his preaching and in his dogmatics. The *Life of Jesus* lectures suggest one potential reason for this preference: Schleiermacher evaluated John as a more reliable historical source than were the synoptic Gospels. It is certainly *not* the case that Schleiermacher simply appropriated Johannine incarnational theology.[2] In particular, he rejected a pre-existent logos Christology, as we saw in his use of logos in *Christian Faith* and in his concern to avoid "docetic" readings (those which attribute consciousness of pre-existence to Christ) in the *Life of Jesus* lectures.[3]

On the other hand, Schleiermacher's portrayal of Christ shares significant characteristics with the Johannine portrayal: Jesus consistently

1. Investigating the possibility that Schleiermacher's preaching strongly influenced the development of his theology belongs to lines of inquiry somewhat different from that of the present study.

2. For one succinct statement of the reading that Schleiermacher appropriated Johannine incarnational theology see Creed, *Divinity of Jesus Christ*, 32–34.

3. In this judgment I explicitly disagree with Wolfgang Trillhaas' claim that one of the two main aspects of Schleiermacher's "Johannine" picture of the Redeemer is the teaching of the pre-existence of the Redeemer. See Trillhaas, *Schleiermachers Predigt*, 189.

expresses his awareness of his special status as the Christ, an awareness grounded in his unique relationship to the Father; also, the teaching and preaching of Jesus are directed toward drawing persons into relationship with him and through him to the Father. How we account for these commonalities depends, in part, on our own readings of John.

I have argued in chapter five that the selection of historical-critical criteria occurs in a theological context. The criteria selected both direct and constrain the evaluation and interpretation of biblical texts. The criterion of continuity that I described Schleiermacher's using directed him toward the expectation that the consciousness of persons of faith in the early Johannine community and the consciousness of Christ himself would be in continuity. On this basis, then, the Johannine portrayal of Christ's discourses might be historically credible in its content, even if not in its form of presentation. If one does *not* accept the criterion of continuity, of course, such a conclusion might appear to be an expression of faith rather than of historical judgment.

The danger for us as we evaluate Schleiermacher's reading of John is that we would treat John as if it had only one historically justifiable interpretation—our own. If we use our own historical-critical reading of John as the standard for what constitutes an "historical" reading of the text, we implicitly insert our own theological presuppositions into the discussion because we consider our criteria to be credible in a particular theological context and because that context is implied when we use the criteria.

What this means as we try to explain why there are commonalities between Schleiermacher's portrayal of Christ and the Johannine portrayal is that there are at least two different potential bases for our explanation. If we disagree with Schleiermacher about the credibility of an historical-critical criterion of continuity, then our explanation of the commonalities between Schleiermacher and John will tend to focus judgmentally upon Schleiermacher's implicit theological reasons for "appropriating" the Johannine portrayal. This is the predominant critical reading of Schleiermacher's position.

On the other hand, if we are willing to entertain the possibility of a criterion of continuity, we have a different basis for our explanation. This basis for explaining the commonalities between Schleiermacher and John accepts the *possibility* of critically using John as an historical source even if interpretation of the reliability of certain details from that source differs significantly from Schleiermacher's interpretation.[4] On this basis, we may say that the commonalities between Schleiermacher's portrayal and the Johannine portrayal are the result of an historical-critical use of the Johannine text even though we may not agree with all of the particular conclusions Schleiermacher drew from this source.

This reading of Schleiermacher suggests that it is not helpful to typify his theology as Johannine, simply because such a typification leaves far too much room for misunderstanding. An author's precise interpretation of what constitutes being Johannine must be provided in order that whatever attribution is to be made will be clear and meaningful.

Potential Implications for Contemporary Use of *Brief Outline* to Organize Theological Studies

In the West in the late twentieth century, we teach the disciplines of preaching, dogmatic or systematic theology, and biblical criticism and interpretation in seminaries and in the academy as if systematic theology and biblical criticism and interpretation provide the sole foundation upon which preaching is to be constructed or the content that preaching is designed to communicate. This type of organization follows the pattern proposed by Schleiermacher in his *Brief Outline*. The goal is always that of serving the church, especially through practical theology. Schleiermacher's organization of theology moves from philosophical theology and historical theology (including biblical studies) to practical theology, including preaching—from the theoretical to its application.

However, as Schleiermacher repeatedly pointed out there, and as we have seen in carefully examining Schleiermacher's practice, the movement is far more interactive than it is a progression in one direction. The presuppositions that significantly shape the issues addressed in his dogmatic theology and that provide a context for the selection of historical-critical criteria emerged early in Schleiermacher's preaching, but that preaching itself began almost exclusively with criticism and interpretation of biblical texts. There was a constant interaction between text, proclamation, and rigorous scholarly analysis and reflection. Because Schleiermacher was preaching at least weekly during most of his career, this interaction was not occasional; it formed the pattern of his week and of his days.

4. Resistance to this possibility among contemporary biblical scholars is strong, as can be seen in the silent dismissive response to John A.T. Robinson's posthumous work, *Priority of John*. Robinson does *not* use a criterion of continuity; he simply entertains the possibility that John might provide some data that might contribute to identifying a historical Jesus.

There is much evidence to indicate that Schleiermacher assumed this context as he wrote *Brief Outline*. If so, then in its broader structure *Brief Outline* provides a somewhat simplified way to think about the more complex practice of theology he advocated there. The more we lose sight of that complex practice as we read *Brief Outline* today, however, the more likely we are to be satisfied with specializations that rarely interact. Schleiermacher's approach is a theology of the church and for the church using the most credible scholarly tools available in the culture. If today we begin, as *Brief Outline* does, with philosophical theology but do so apart from a context of constant interaction between biblical text, proclamation, and reflection, we will not be using Schleiermacher's actual method. We will have adopted one aspect of Schleiermacher's organization of theology while ignoring his definition of its nature and purpose in relation to communities of faith. The questions arise: Is that organization of theology dependent upon his own model of interactive practice? Why should the various disciplines in the study of Christianity continue to be organized in the pattern of *Brief Outline* if the premise behind that organization is not maintained?

This reading of Schleiermacher's practice invites us to continue to evaluate contemporary use of *Brief Outline*. What we may not do with integrity is to assume that Schleiermacher's context was primarily an academic one. Schleiermacher's dogmatic and historical-critical work was informed by and responsive to his preaching to and on behalf of the community of faith.

Theological Method: Faith and History

Dietz Lange has argued persuasively that Schleiermacher understood Christianity to be defined between two poles: faith or piety on the one side and history investigated critically on the other.[5] It is clear in Schleiermacher's use and interpretation of John that he was building a way to relate faith and history. This approach is different both from pre-Enlightenment orthodoxy's claim that faith's description *is* historical, and from twentieth century neo-orthodoxy's claim that faith and history are incommensurate realms, which cannot be closely related without compromising the truth of faith. For Schleiermacher, the link holding faith and history together is pious Christian experience. Because of this experience it is possible to account for Christ simultaneously as an object of faith and as an historical figure. Since pious Christian experience is the meeting point between

5. Lange, *Historischer Jesus*.

faith and history, it follows that the experience itself may illuminate the nature of Christ as the object both of faith and of historical investigation. Chapter four's use of a preaching experience illustrated the role such experience might have had in the construction of Schleiermacher's dogmatics.

Schleiermacher's practice of using historical criticism and pious Christian experience as the boundaries for thinking about Christianity provides a potentially useful model for relating contemporary historical Jesus research and the Christological enterprise. I would like to suggest an alternative, however, to the visual image Schleiermacher himself used to describe the relation of faith and history. Schleiermacher's image was of two poles, perhaps like the ends of a magnet, or perhaps like endpoints for a line segment. I find it more useful to visualize Schleiermacher's relating of faith and history with a different geometric image—a graph defined by an x axis and a y axis.

In geometry, two lines, the x axis and the y axis, intersect through a point and together define a planar field. Everything on the plane can be located by using the two axes to provide coordinates. To visualize Schleiermacher's thought, we might define the x axis as a series of pictures of Jesus that is developed through historical-critical research. Similarly, the y axis might be defined as a series of expressions of Christian experience. These two axes define a field—Christianity.

Now, if we play with this visual image of a graph, several things become obvious. An attempt to use only one axis to define the field results in a one-dimensional definition—a line. It is possible to describe the field as a whole or to locate a single point on it only in relation to *both* historical research and Christian piety. Everything in Christianity, including the positions of the various biblical texts, can be located on such a graph through the use of two coordinates, one historical-critical and the other a form of piety. Such a metaphorical mapping of Christianity encourages interpretation of events and expressions both in relation to each other and in relation to later events and expressions. We might push the metaphor further to speculate that the point of intersection between the axes is the historical Jesus. Both axes are in direct continuity with that one point; both historical criticism and piety are in continuity with Jesus. The metaphor highlights the relative uselessness of setting one's goal as that of identifying the singular, unique historical Jesus. A single point has no dimension and no ability to help us to place anything else in relationship to it apart from the axes used to define it. An infinite number of fields can be run through a single point; two axes are required to define a particular planar field. So, the graph metaphor suggests that the historical Jesus alone, apart from the interpretations of historical research and from expressions of pious Christian experience, is insufficient to define or interpret Christianity. It is in relation to both the series of historical-critical investigations that interpret Jesus and his effects and the series of expressions of Christian piety that manifest faith in him and his power as Redeemer that Christianity is defined and adequately interpreted. This visual image of Schleiermacher's effort to relate faith and history emphasizes how they overlap completely in order to coordinate usefully. This interaction is expressly clear in Schleiermacher's various uses of the Gospel of John.

Theological Method: The Interrelationships between Preaching, Dogmatics, and Biblical Criticism

A complex interaction between Schleiermacher's preaching, dogmatics, and biblical criticism has become evident as a result of examining his use of the Gospel of John. The presuppositions that provided a context for the selection of criteria in biblical criticism emerged early in Schleiermacher's preaching and remained consistent throughout it. The contextualization of those same presuppositions within a systematic exposition was a major achievement of the dogmatics, and the experience of preaching itself provided insight into the development of the dogmatic picture of redemption.

The complexity of the interaction between Schleiermacher's preaching, dogmatics, and biblical criticism indicated by this study suggests that the fruitfulness of reading his thought by beginning with his preaching has not been exhausted.

The picture of Schleiermacher's thought that has been developed here is significantly different from that which emerges for readers who begin with *Christian Faith*, with its propositions borrowed in part from philosophical theology. Brian Gerrish's characterization is typical for that view: ". . . the whole of [Schleiermacher's] theology can best be seen as moving between two points: a specifically Christian relationship with Christ and a universally human consciousness of God."[6] In direct contrast to that view, the picture which has been drawn by beginning with Schleiermacher's preaching makes clearer the *borrowing* of concepts from philosophical theology to articulate an understanding, the actual source of which lies elsewhere—in the life of the church. The picture leads us to ask whether the weaknesses in Schleiermacher's philosophical and historical account of God-consciousness as appearing at a particular stage of human development and pointing to a possibly universal human appropriation of it might

6. Gerrish, *Prince of the Church*, 23.

arise because he began with an analogy between a *Christian's* consciousness and Christ's consciousness and then generalized from that point toward an ideal condition. If this is the case, the most interesting questions are theological rather than philosophical.

My suggestion that a particular experience might underlie Schleiermacher's description of the sanctified life and by extension the perfect life of Christ leads us to question the common assessment that Schleiermacher's theology is based upon a transcendental deduction from human experience in general. It is possible to read the Introduction to *Christian Faith* as an appropriation of concepts in order to have a language in which the experience introduced in chapter four can be intelligibly described among persons of faith in general within a given faith community and used to describe the person of Christ in particular. Schleiermacher clearly indicated that the ordering of *Christian Faith* was somewhat arbitrary and was selected in part to match the traditional organization of theological topics. However, if Christ is truly the realization of ideal human life in history, then the sanctified life, in which redeemed humans come to approach that ideal human life in their own histories, is the location for drawing an analogy between Christ and believers. I have suggested that one particular experience is a way of thinking concretely about the source of that analogy as Schleiermacher described it.

Schleiermacher used a theory of ideality (*Urbildlichkeit*) to explain the communication of redemption/sanctification to believers. Can contemporary theologians set aside that particular theory of communication and yet still follow Schleiermacher in beginning to understand Christ as the location of the experience of sanctified life, using theories of communication or transformation that are credible in our own contexts? Or is the use of an analogy between Christ and persons of faith meaningful only in relation to Schleiermacher's theory? Such questions invite us to our own constructions of Christology out of and for our own communities of faith.

Three Nodal Points for Developing Christology

In a highly simplified description of the bases for Schleiermacher's Christology, three nodal points emerge: first, a set of theological presuppositions that we identified as having emerged in his preaching; second, an experience of being a vehicle of the divine presence, which is used as the point of analogy between Christ and persons of faith; and third, a theory about how change in persons is evoked (Schleiermacher's theory of the function of this "*Urbild*" and its power to evoke itself). This third nodal point has been present in our description of Schleiermacher's work but has necessarily not been a primary focus of it.[7]

One of the results of describing Schleiermacher's Christology in terms of these three nodes is that they make very clear that his methodological approach to Christology does not require him to be dependent upon the Gospel of John. He *does* rely heavily upon some aspects of John in his own execution of his method, but the method itself does not require this dependence. This observation is consistent with the argument in chapter five that Schleiermacher worked with the Gospel of John as an historical source.

It seems to me that one might fruitfully follow Schleiermacher's lead in the construction of a dogmatic Christology for a community of faith by consciously identifying and working with those three nodal points as they exist or are described in that community. For the first node one might work with preachers to identify the operating presuppositions undergirding their preaching. The second node would involve articulation of an experience that may be used as a point of analogy between Christ and persons of faith. Finally, the third node would be a development or appropriation of a theory of personal and social transformation, how it happens and what triggers it. A Christology for and by a feminist community, for example, would turn to feminist preaching, an experience that is articulated in feminist communities, and feminist theories of transformation and liberation. A Christology for and by an evangelical community would turn to evangelical preaching, an experience articulated in evangelical communities and theories associated with conversion. Very likely, the content of these two resulting Christologies would be significantly different, and it is possible that the results in some communities of faith would obscure the idea of beginning from an articulation of the three nodes in the first place. This approach to Christology makes the most sense, perhaps, in pietist contexts where the expectation is that redemption involves both personal interaction between persons of faith and the divine and that Christian communities provide essential interpretation of the experience identified as redemption.

As an example for us today, Schleiermacher invites theologians to begin our work in the location where we are most confident that the Spirit is operative: in worshipping communities. This is also the challenge Karl Barth placed before us in his emphasis upon the Word which comes to us. What distinguishes Schleiermacher's example from Barth's is Schleier-

7. For a careful and thorough study of *Urbildlichkeit* in Schleiermacher's dogmatics, see Maureen Junker, *Urbild des Gottesbewußtseins.*

macher's utter confidence that faith and history overlap and coordinate. The description of this common space is neither simple nor easy. Yet, a doctrine of incarnation is indistinguishable from an ecstatic utterance if it is not possible to describe this space reflectively and critically.

Schleiermacher was always aware that as theologians we speak within living faith traditions, rearticulating them for our contexts and ourselves. Like Schleiermacher, we articulate to the best of our ability the truth that we live, knowing that we have not captured the whole of it for time and eternity. He dared to speak, as we do, because he trusted that as he opened himself to becoming a vehicle for more than he knew, assimilating to Christ, more than he himself and his partial truth would become manifest.

Appendix A

A Listing of Schleiermacher's Preaching on Texts from the Gospel of John, Arranged by Biblical Text

This study is based upon a reading of all of the published sermons on Johannine texts and many but by no means all of the manuscript outlines and transcriptions that have survived. The de Gruyter publishing house archive had a cabinet with approximately 700 manuscripts that were both uncatalogued and unavailable as I was doing archival research there in 1995. The Schleiermacher Forschungstelle in Kiel has since catalogued these items and will be making that listing available in the near future. This appendix, therefore, is a partial listing of Schleiermacher's preaching on John. It is a complete listing of the preaching upon which my judgments are based.

In this list, citations that do not have either manuscript or publication data are citations from the unpublished daily diaries, access to which I obtained through the careful notes of Wolfgang Virmond of the Schleiermacherforschungstelle, Berlin. Manuscript transcriptions or outlines are identified by SN #, and are found in the Schleiermacher Nachlass of the Akadamie der Wissenschaften in Berlin. Manuscripts in the de Gruyter Archive are specifically noted. Publication data are provided for the published version of sermons used in this study. A complete listing of the publication history of each published sermon is found in Meding, *Bibliographie der Schriften Schleiermachers* (Schleiermacher-Archiv 9; Berlin: de Gruyter, 1992). The published sermon number (P###) assigned by Meding is provided to assist the reader in making reference to that bibliography. When a manuscript exists for a published sermon, both are listed. Not provided for purposes of this study is Terrence N. Tice's listing and placing in context of all these sermons in the order in which they were originally preached. See his book *Schleiermacher's Sermons* (Lewiston, NY: Mellen, 1997).

Calendar citations are provided in the German order: date.month.year. The Latin names for some Sundays before and after Easter were used by Schleiermacher. The numbers before season names should be read as follows: 2 Advent = Second Sunday in Advent; 2 Weihnachten = the Sunday after Christmas; 4 Epiphany = Fourth Sunday after Epiphany; 20 Trinitatis = Twentieth Sunday after Trinity Sunday = Twenty-first Sunday in Trinity.

Hauptpredigt is the main Sunday morning service sermon. *Frühpredigt* is the early Sunday morning sermon. *Nachmittag* is the Sunday afternoon service. *Vorbereitung* is the Saturday service, usually a confessional service in preparation for Sunday.

A *Nachschrift* is a transcription of a sermon by a person in the congregation. It may have been written down during the preaching or at some time later. An *Entwurf* is a sermon outline by Schleiermacher himself, written before or after the preaching. *Tagebücher* are the daily diaries that Schleiermacher kept for his own records. The collection of these that has survived is incomplete.

This listing is ordered by biblical text rather than by chronology in order to draw attention to patterns in Schleiermacher's use of the Gospel across his preaching career.

Sermons in the series preached in 1823–1827 are starred (*).

Summary Statistics

The question of how to count the number of John sermons is complicated because of the variety of sources and the overlapping of sources. I have counted two or more forms or records of a particular sermon on a date as one sermon unless there are indications that a sermon was preached twice on that date.

In all, 95 sermons comprise the "John series" from April 13,1823 to May 20,1827, 74 of which were published in SW II/8 & 9 (John 1:1—16:33); 8 additional Nachschriften for unpublished sermons exist (John 17:1—18:38); 9 more Nachschriften for published sermons also exist (John 14:7—16:33), and these duplicate published Nachschriften but differ considerably. Thirteen dates and biblical texts for the remainder of the series are specified in the *Tagebücher*. So, of the 95 sermons preached in the series on John we have Nachschriften for 82, and the biblical text and date for all 95.

Thus far, 55 sermons on Johannine texts were published in addition to those just noted in the series on John. In addition there are 14 *Entwürfe* of unpublished sermons on Johannine texts, 18 *Nachschriften* of unpublished sermons on Johannine texts, and 54 Notations regarding known sermons on Johannine texts for which there is no sermon text, *Entwurf* or *Nachschrift*.

When all these categories are sorted out, there are a total of 228 occasions we now know about on which Schleiermacher preached on a text from the Gospel of John.

Biblical Text	Date Preached	Sunday in Church Year	Published Sermon Number, Sermon Title (if titled), Publication Data, or Manuscript Data
John ?	11.5.1828	Rogate Hauptpredigt	
John ?	21.3.1830	Laetare Hauptpredigt	
John 1: ?	3.2.1822	4 Epiphany	
*John 1:1–5	13.4.1823	Misericordias Domini	P362; 1837; SW II/8, 3–14
*John 1:6–12	4.5.1823	Rogate	P363; 1837; SW II/8, 15–28
John 1: 12–17	5.12.1830	2 Advent	P137; Hauptpredigt; 1835, SWII/4, 195–208; first published in 1831
*John 1:14–18	11.5.1823	Exaudi	P364; 1837; SW II/8, 29–42
John 1:14	26.12.1814	Weihnachten Montag	Manuscript in de Gruyter archive: Pishon Ns (A transcription by Pishon corrected by Schleiermacher)
John 1:14	8.3.1829	Invocavit Hauptpredigt	

Biblical Text	Date Preached	Sunday in Church Year	Published Sermon Number, Sermon Title (if titled), Publication Data, or Manuscript Data
*John 1:19–24(5)	1.6.1823	1 Trinitatis	P365; 1837; SW II/8, 43–54
John 1:19–28	before 1833		P210; "Johannes' Zeugnis von Christo, ein vorbild des unsrigen." 1834; SW II/2, 284–88
John 1:23–27	22.12.1833	4 Advent	P231 (The daily diary lists this sermon text as on John 1:22) 1835; SW II/3, 724–37
*John 1:24–28	15.6.1823	3 Trinitatis	P366; 1837; SW II/8, 55–67
*John 1:29–34	29.6.1823	5 Trinitatis	P367; 1837; SW II/8, 68–84
*John 1:35–42	13.7.1823	7 Trinitatis	P368; Manuscript in de Gruyter archive 1837; SW II/8, 85–99
John 1:35–44	1810	Season of Epiphany	P360; "Welche wichtige Bemerkungen und Wahrheiten wir uns aus dieser Wahl des Erlösers, durch welche er sich den ersten Jüngerkreis bildete, ableiten können." 1836; SW II/7, 575–79

Biblical Text	Date Preached	Sunday in Church Year	Published Sermon Number, Sermon Title (if titled), Publication Data, or Manuscript Data
John 1:35–51	5.1.1812	2 Weihnachten	P33; "Das Zusammentreten Christi und seiner Jünger, ein Vorbild, wie wir ernste gesellige Verhältnisse ansuknüpfen haben." 1834; SW II/1, 387–99 (full sermon text); 1908, Bauer 355–56 (outline of sermon from Schleiermacher's manuscript now lost)
*John 1:43–51	27.7.1823	9 Trinitatis	P369; 1837; SW II/8, 100–111
John 1:45ff	20.12.1795	4 Advent	P565; Nachmittag "Einige Vorsichtsmaßregeln bei der Wahl unserer Freunde." Am 4. Advent 1795, in Landsberg. SN 51: 89–90 (outline by Schleiermacher). 1908; Bauer 353–54
John 1:46	9.12.1827	2.Advent	Hauptpredigt; The following three lines are recorded in the daily diary: "Das der Glaube; I. in allgemein der Fortgang desselben; II. in besonderen das wir"
John 1:47–51	15.1.1832	2 Epiphany	P166; "Wie sich das Verhältnis zwischen dem Erlöser und seinem Jünger Nathanael gestaltete." 1835; SW II/3, 156–68

Biblical Text	Date Preached	Sunday in Church Year	Published Sermon Number, Sermon Title (if titled), Publication Data, or Manuscript Data
John 2: ?	17.2.1822	6 Epiphany	
John 2:1–11	18.1.1807	2 Epiphany	P22; "Was das Edlere in der Welt sich aus dem Niedrigen entwikkelt." 1834; SW II/1, 298–311
*John 2:1–11	19.10.1823	21 Trinitatis	P370; 1837; SW II/8, 112–27
*John 2:12–17	2.11.1823	23 Trinitatis	P371; 1837; SW II/8, 128–41
John 2:13–16	15.1.1826	2 Epiphany	Hauptpredigt Manuscript in the de Gruyter archive: Sethe 1826a p.57 (A notebook of transcriptions of Schleiermacher's preaching written by Sethe)
John 2:13–17	1810	Season of Epiphany	P361; "Die Gründzuge nach denen unser Erlöser bei Verbesserung alles dessen, was auf die religiöse Verbindung der Menschen Zuzug hat, zu Werke ging" 1836; SW II/7, 579–83
*John 2:18–25	16.11.1823	25 Trinitatis	P372; 1837; SW II/8, 142–54
John 3:1ff	31.5.1795	Trinitatis	SN 51: 64 (outline by Schleiermacher)
*John 3:1–16	30.11.1823	1 Advent	P373; 1837; SW II/8, 155–67

Biblical Text	Date Preached	Sunday in Church Year	Published Sermon Number, Sermon Title (if titled), Publication Data, or Manuscript Data
John 3:1–8	24.5.1812	Trinitatis	P41; "Daß der Mensch nur durch die neue Geburt in das Reich Gottes kommt. Trinitatis." 1834; SW II/1, 492–509
John 3:6	25.5.1828	Pfingsten	Frühpredigt
*John 3:7–15	14.12.1823	3 Advent	P374; 1837; SW II/8, 168–84
John 3:8	4.6.1797	Pfingsten	Nachmittag; SN 52: 29–30 (outline by Schleiermacher)
John 3:10	11.6.1797	Oster	SN 52: 31 (outline by Schleiermacher)
John 3:14–15	24.3.1826	Charfreitag	Hauptpredigt; Manuscript in de Gruyter archive: Sethe 1826a p.141
*John 3:16–18	25.12.1823	Weihnachten	P375; 1837; SW II/8, 185–96
*John 3:19–21	28.12.1823	Sunday after Weihnachten	P376; 1837; SW II/8, 197–206
John 3:20–21	30.12.1821	1 Weihnachten	
*John 3:22–30	4.1.1824	Sunday after New Year	P377; 1837; SW II/8, 207–18
*John 3:31–36	18.1.1824	2 Epiphany	P378; 1837; SW II/8, 219–31
*John 4:1–10	1.2.1824	4 Epiphany	P379; 1837; SW II/8, 232–48

Biblical Text	Date Preached	Sunday in Church Year	Published Sermon Number, Sermon Title (if titled), Publication Data, or Manuscript Data
John 4:4–26	19.1.1812	2 Epiphany	P34; SN 592–95 (transcription not in Schleiermacher's hand) "Das Verfahren des Erlösers in seinem Gespräch mit der Samariterin." 1834; SW II/1, 400–413
*John 4:11–19	15.2.1824	Septuagesimae	P380; 1837; SW II/8, 249–62
*John 4:20–24	14.3.1824	Reminiscere	P381; 1837; SW II/8, 263–78
John 4:25–26	29.1.1832	4 Epiphany	P167; "Das Gespräch Christi mit der Samariterin nach seinem eigentlichen Inhalt und der Belehrung Christi, der darin liegt. Am 4. Sonntage nach Epiphany 1832"; 1835/23 SW II/3, 169–80
*John 4:25–34	28.3.1824	Laetare	P382; 1837; SW II/8, 279–90
*John 4:35–42	11.4.1824	Palmarum	P383; 1837; SW II/8, 291–302
*John 4:43–54	9.5.1824	Jubilate	P384; 1837; SW II/8, 303–15
*John 5:1–15	16.5.1824	Kantate	P385; 1837; SW II/8, 316–30
John 5:5–16	1794	Trinitatiszeit	P332; "Wie übel es ist dasjenige nicht verschweigen zu können, was uns zu reden verboten ist." 1836; SW II/7, 290–301

Biblical Text	Date Preached	Sunday in Church Year	Published Sermon Number, Sermon Title (if titled), Publication Data, or Manuscript Data
*John 5:16–23	13.6.1824	Trinitatis	P386; 1837; SW II/8, 331–46
*John 5:24–30	27.6.1824	2 Trinitatis	P387; 1837; SW II/8, 347–64
*John 5:31–40	11.7.1824	4 Trinitatis	P388; 1837; SW II/8, 365–79
*John 5:41–47	25.7.1824	6 Trinitatis	P389; 1837; SW II/8, 380–91
John 6: ?	8.7.1820	6 Trinitatis	Vorbereitspredigt
*John 6:1–15	8.8.1824	8 Trinitatis	P390; 1837; SW II/8, 392–401
*John 6:16–25	17.10.1824	18 Trinitatis	P391; 1837; SW II/8, 402–15
*John 6:27–35	31.10.1824	20 Trinitatis	P392; 1837; SW II/8, 416–29
*John 6:36–44	14.11.1824	22 Trinitatis	P393; 1837; SW II/8, 430–42
John 6:39–40	23.11.1823	Todtenfest	P74; Hauptpredigt "Trost und Freude in Bezug auf unsere Entschlafenen." 1835; SW II/4, 353–65; English translation: 1987, DeVries, *Servant of the Word*, 196–208
*John 6:45–51	28.11.1824	1 Advent	P394; 1837; SW II/8, 443–54
*John 6:52–60	12.12.1824	3 Advent	P395; 1837; SW II/8, 455–67
*John 6:61–71	9.1.1825	1 Epiphany	P396; 1837; SW II/8, 468–75
John 6:67	7.6.1828	1 Trinitatis	Vorbereitungspredigt

Biblical Text	Date Preached	Sunday in Church Year	Published Sermon Number, Sermon Title (if titled), Publication Data, or Manuscript Data
*John 7:1–13	6.2.1825	Sexagesimä	P397; 1847; SW II/9, 1–15
John 7:10ff	16.2.1812	Invocavit	SN 592–39 (transcription not in Schleiermacher's hand)
*John 7:14–24	20.2.1825	Invocavit	P398; 1847; SW II/9, 16–31
John 7:18	2.1.1825	2 Weihnachten	P96; Hauptpredigt; "Christus, der Lehrer." 1835; SW II/4, 546–56, first published in 1826
*John 7:25–36	6.3.1825	Oculi	P399; 1847; SW II/9, 32–45
*John 7:37–53	20.3.1825	Judica	P400; 1847; SW II/9, 46–63
John 7:40–53	16.2.1812	Invocavit	P36; "Von dem Vorurtheile des Buchstabens und dem Vorurtheile des Ansehns." 1834; SW II/1, 425–36
*John 8:12–20	17.4.1825	Misericordias Domini	P401; 1847; SW II/9, 64–81
*John 8:20–29	8.5.1825	Rogate	P402; 1847; SW II/9, 82–94
*John 8:30–38	15.5.1825	Exaudi	P403; 1847; SW II/9, 95–107
John 8:31–32	21.7.1822	5 Trinitatis	Waisenhauskirche, exchange with Herzberg

Biblical Text	Date Preached	Sunday in Church Year	Published Sermon Number, Sermon Title (if titled), Publication Data, or Manuscript Data
John 8:37	2.11.1794	20 Trinitatis	P334; SN 51: 19a (outline) "Von den billigen Grenzen unsrer Abneigung gegen diejenigen, welche von einer ganz andern Verfassung des Gemüths sind, als wir. Ueber John 8:37." 1836; SW II/7, 314–27
*John 8:39–45	5.6.1825	1 Trinitate	P404; 1847; SW II/9, 108–22
*John 8:46–59	19.6.1825	3 Trinitate	P405; 1847; SW II/9, 123–37
John 8:51	24.11.1827	Totenfest	Vorbereitungspredigt; "Unser Glaube das von Christu das Leben ist."
John 8:56	27.11.1831	1 Advent	P161; Am 1. Sonntage des Advents, 1831; 1834, SW II/2, 271–83
*John 9:1–7	17.7.1825	7 Trinitate	P406; 1847; SW II/9, 138–52
*John 9:8–23	31.7.1825	9 Trinitate	P407; 1847; SW II/9, 153–67
*John 9:24–41	14.8.1825	11 Trinitate	P408; 1847; SW II/9, 168–83
John 9:35–38	12.2.1832	6 Epiphany	P168; "Wie durch unsern Herrn und Erlöser die Werke Gottes und dem Blindgebornen sind offenbar beworden." 1835; SW II/3, 181–94
John 10: ?	17.4.1831	Misericordias Domini	Schwerinsburg (presumably guest preaching)

Biblical Text	Date Preached	Sunday in Church Year	Published Sermon Number, Sermon Title (if titled), Publication Data, or Manuscript Data
*John 10:1–11	28.8.1825	13 Trinitate	P409; 1847; SW II/9, 184–97
*John 10:12–21	11.9.1825	15 Trinitate	P410; 1847; SW II/9, 198–212
John 10:16	20.4.1828	Misericordias Domini	Hauptpredigt
John 10:17–18	31.3.1809	Charfreytage	P30; "Wie es auch für uns ein Ruhm ist und ein Vorzug, wenn wir macht haben, unser Leben zu lassen." Am Charfreytage. Nachmittags. Dreifaltigkeitskirche. 1835; SW II/4, 778–81
John 10:17–18	12.4.1811	Karfreitag	
*John 10:22–33	9.10.1825	19 Trinitate	P411; 1847; SW II/9, 213–25
*John 10:34–42	23.10.1825	21 Trinitate	P412; 1847; SW II/9, 226–37
John 11: ?	3.4.1831	Ostern	Hauptpredigt
*John 11:1–14	6.11.1825	23 Trinitate	P413; 1847; SW II/9, 238–50
John 11:13f and 19:3f	27.4.1828	Jubilate	Frühpredigt
*John 11:15–27	20.11.1825	Todtenfeste	P414; 1847; SW II/9, 251–63
John 11:16	25.11.1832	Todtenfest	P192; Hauptpredigt "Vorshcriften für den Schmerz be idem Verlust unserer Brüder. Am Todtenfeste, 1832." 1834; SW II/2, 598–609

Biblical Text	Date Preached	Sunday in Church Year	Published Sermon Number, Sermon Title (if titled), Publication Data, or Manuscript Data
*John 11:28–40	4.12.1825	2 Advent	P415; 1847; SW II/9, 264–76
*John 11:41–54	18.12.1825	4 Advent	P416; 1847; SW II/9, 277–91
*John 11:53—12:8	8.1.1826	1 Epiphany	P417; 1847; SW II/9, 292–304
*John 12:9–19	22.1.1826	Septuagesimä	P418; 1847; SW II/9, 305–19
*John 12:20–26	5.2.1826	Estomihi	P419; 1847; SW II/9, 320–32
John 12:24	27.3.1807	Karfreitag	Bauer, *patriotischer Prediger*, 44, gives this reference and indicates that the sermon is not published.
John 12:24	22.2.1818	Oculi	Hauptpredigt; Nachschrift in deGruyter Archive, identifying label unknown.
John 12:24	20.2.1820	Invocavit	(Hauptpredigt?)
John 12:26	1.1.1828	Neujahr	Hauptpredigt
*John 12:27–36	19.2.1826	Reminiscere	P420; 1847; SW II/9, 333–47
John 12:32	19.3.1820	Judica	
*John 12:36–43	5.3.1826	Laetare	P421; 1847; SW II/9, 348–61
*John 12:44–50	19.3.1826	Palmarum	P422; 1847; SW II/9, 362–75
*John 13:1–11	2.4.1826	Quasimodo-geniti	P423; 1847; SW II/9, 376–88
John 13:8	before 1828		P129; Beichtrede. 1835; SW II/4, 805–807

Biblical Text	Date Preached	Sunday in Church Year	Published Sermon Number, Sermon Title (if titled), Publication Data, or Manuscript Data
*John 13:12–20	16.4.1826	Jubilate	P424; 1847; SW II/9, 389–98
*John 13:21–38	23.4.1826	Cantate	P425; 1847; SW II/9, 399–416
John 13:31–35	13.3.1831	Laetare	Hauptpredigt; Bauer, *Ungedruckte Predigten*, 124, gives this reference.
John 13:34	10.2.1833	Sexagesima	P199; "Wie durch die Liebe des Erlösers zu uns auch schon unsre brüderliche Gemeinschaft unter einander gegründet wurde und erhalten ble-ibt. Am 4. Sonntage nach Epiphanias 1833." 1835; SW II/3, 470–482; von Meding remarks: "Im Jahr 1833 gab es keinen 4. Sonntag nach Epiphanias. Schleiermachers Termin-kalender belegt John13:34 als Predigttext des Sonn-tags Sexagesimä (10.2.1833)." English translation: 1987; DeVries, *Servant of the Word*, 215–27.
John 13:35	14.10.1797	18 Trinitatis	Vorbereitung; SN 52: 45–46 (outline in Schleiermacher's hand)
John 13:35	5.5.1819	Bußbettage	(This was a Prussian day of prayer, the Wednesday after Jubilate.)

Biblical Text	Date Preached	Sunday in Church Year	Published Sermon Number, Sermon Title (if titled), Publication Data, or Manuscript Data
*John 14:1–6	4.5.1826	Himmelfahrtstage	P426; 1847; SW II/9, 417–27
*John 14:7–17	21.5.1826	Trinitatis	P427; Manuscript in de Gruyter archive: Sethe 1826b: 1–11; 1847; SW II/9, 428–42
John 14:9	13.2.1831	6 Epiphany	Hauptpredigt
John 14:9	27.5.1832	Rogate	P177; "Was für einen Gewinn wir von der rechten Betrachtung des Erlösers haben sollen und können. Am 5. Sonntage nach Ostern, 1832." 1835; SW II/3, 265–75
*John 14:18–24	4.6.1826	2 Trinitatis	P428; Manuscript in de Gruyter archive: Sethe, 1826b: 24–35; 1847; SW II/9, 443–56
John 14:23–26	15.5.1796	Pfingsten	SN 51: 128–29 (outline in Schleiermacher's hand)
*John 14:25–31	18.6.1826	4 Trinitatis	P429; Manuscript in de Gruyter archive: Sethe, 1826b: 47–56; 1847; SW II/9, 457–68
John 14:27	12.6.1831	2 Trinitatis	P140; Hauptpredigt; "Wie jedes einzelne Gemüth in dem Frieden des Erlösers eine unendliche Fülle der göttlichen Weisheit erkennt. Am 2. Sonntag nach Trinitatis 1831." 1835; SW II/3, 1–10

Biblical Text	Date Preached	Sunday in Church Year	Published Sermon Number, Sermon Title (if titled), Publication Data, or Manuscript Data
John 14:30–31	25.3.1832	Oculi	P171; "Die Gesinnung in welcher Christus seinem Leiden entgegenging. Am Sonntag Oculi 1832." 1834; SW II/2, 417–29
*John 15:1–7	2.7.1826	6 Trinitatis	P430; Manuscript in de Gruyter archive: Sethe, 1826b: 70–85; 1847; SW II/9, 469–83
*John 15:8–17	16.7.1826	8 Trinitatis	P431; Manuscript in de Gruyter archive: Sethe 1826b: 94–104; 1847; SW II/9, 484–94
John 15:9, 14–15	17.8.1806	11 Trinitatis	P16; SN 56–4 (outline) "Daß wir nicht Knechte Gottes sein sollen sondern Freunde." 1834, SW II/1, 208–222 (full text); 1908, Bauer, 325–27 (accurate transcription of outline)
John 15:14	13.11.1831	24 Trinitatis	P150; "Das Eigenthümliche in den Verhältniß des Herrn zu seinen Jüngern, daß sie seine Freunde sind gerade wegen ihres Gehorsams. Am 24. Sonntage nach Trinitatis 1831." 1835; SW II/3, 107–20

Biblical Text	Date Preached	Sunday in Church Year	Published Sermon Number, Sermon Title (if titled), Publication Data, or Manuscript Data
John 15:15	28.5.1797	Exaudi	P554; "Unser Beruf, Freunde Gottes zu werden." SN 52: 28–29 (outline) "Am Sonntag Exaudi 1797 in Berlin," Hauptpredigt; 1908 Bauer 323 (accurate transcription of outline)
John 15:15	16.8.1802		P555; "Unser Beruf Freunde Gottes zu sein." SN 54–32 (outline) Am Montag den 16. August 1802 in Stemnitz; 1908 Bauer 323–24 (accurate transcription of outline)
John 15:16	8.2.1824	5 Epiphany	Hauptpredigt
John 15:16	13.2.1825	6 Epiphany	P99; "Christus unter seinen Jüngern." 1835; SW II/4, 586–601
*John 15:18—16:4	30.7.1826	10 Trinitatis	P432; Manuscript in de Gruyter archive: Sethe 1826b: 117–27; 1847; SW II/9, 495–509
John 15:26ff	18.5.1828	Exaudi	Hauptpredigt
John 16:1–?	26.5.1816	Exaudi	Manuscript of transcription in de Gruyter archive: Ns Jonas 1816; f14
*John 16:4–15	13.8.1826	12 Trinitatis	P433; Manuscript in de Gruyter archive: Sethe 1826b: 142–52; 1847; SW II/9, 510–23

Biblical Text	Date Preached	Sunday in Church Year	Published Sermon Number, Sermon Title (if titled), Publication Data, or Manuscript Data
John 16:5–7	14.5.1795		P568; SN 51: 60–61 (outline in Schleiermacher's hand) "Die Nothwendigkeit des Hingangs Jesu zum Vater." Predigtentwurf für Himmelfahrt 1795; 1909 Bauer 31–32 (accurate transcription of outline)
John 16:7	5.3.1820	Oculi	
John 16:7	18.5.1823	Pfingsten	Hauptpredigt
John 16:12–15	6.6.1824	Pfingsten	Frühpredigt
John 16:13–14	22.5.1831	Pfingsten	Hauptpredigt
John 16:13–14	11.6.1832		P179; "Wie der Geist der Wahrheit den Erlöser verklärt. Am zweiten Pfingsttage 1832." 1834; SW II/2, 549–61
John 16:14	25.5.1795	2 Pfingsttag	P493; SN 51: 62–63 (outline in Schleiermacher's hand) "Was Christum verklärt und sonst nichts gehört zur christlichen Wahrheit." 1882 Zimmer 369–70 (significant errors or omissions in this transcription of the manuscript outline)
*John 16:16–23	27.8.1826	14 Trinitatis	P434; Manuscript in de Gruyter archive: Sethe 1826b: 161–70; 1847; SW II/9, 524–36

Biblical Text	Date Preached	Sunday in Church Year	Published Sermon Number, Sermon Title (if titled), Publication Data, or Manuscript Data
*John 16:23–33	24.9.1826	18 Trinitatis	P435; Manuscript in de Gruyter archive: Sethe 1826b: 183–93; 1847; SW II/9, 537–48
John 16:23	29.5.1791	Rogate	P311; "Vom rechten Gebet des Christen im Namen Jesu." 1836; SW II/7, 27–41
John 16:24–30	7.5.1820	Rogate	P69; "Ueber die Erhörung des Gebetes im Namen Jesu." According to the daily diary, preached twice, in the Nicolaikirche and in the afternoon in Dreifaltigkeitskirche. 1835; SW II/4, 307–20
John 16:27	11.12.1831	3 Advent	P162; "Wie der Erlöser derjenige ist, um dessentwillen auch wer von Gott beliebt warden. Am 3. Sonntage des Advents 1831." 1835; SW II/3, 121–31
John 16:28	15.5.1828	Himmelfahrt	Frühpredigt
John 16:32	1.4.1832	Laetare	P172; Parochialkirche "Von der Einsamkeit des Erlösers bei seinen Leiden. Am Sonntag Laetare 1832." 1835; SW II/3, 220–28
John 16:33	24.4.1825	Jubilate	Hauptpredigt

Biblical Text	Date Preached	Sunday in Church Year	Published Sermon Number, Sermon Title (if titled), Publication Data, or Manuscript Data
John 16:33	8.4.1832	Judica	P173; "Wie die Ermunterung des Erlösers, daß seiner Jünger sollten getrost sein, unerachtet sie würden Noth haben in der Welt, mit seinem Leiden and Tode zusammenhänge. Am 5. Sonntage in der Fasten, Judica 1832." 1835; SW II/3, 229–41
*John 17:1–8	8.10.1826	20 Trinitatis	Frühpredigt; Manuscript in de Gruyter archive: Sethe 1826b: 204–16
*John 17:9–13	22.10.1826	22 Trinitatis	Manuscript in de Gruyter archive: Sethe 1826b: 235
*John 17:14–19	5.11.1826	24 Trinitatis	
John 17:20–21	24.5.1795	Pfingsten	SN 51: 61–62 (outline in Schleiermacher's hand)
John 17:20–21	7.2.1802	5 Epiphany	SN 54–55 (outline in Schleiermacher's hand)
John 17:20–23	9.6.1821	Sonnabend vor Pfingsten Vorbereitung Einsegnung (Confirmation)	
*John 17:20–24	19.11.1826	26 Trinitatis	
*John 17:24–26	17.12.1826	3 Advent	Manuscript in de Gruyter archive: Sethe 1827a: 16

Biblical Text	Date Preached	Sunday in Church Year	Published Sermon Number, Sermon Title (if titled), Publication Data, or Manuscript Data
John 17:24	22.5.1800	Himmelfahrt	P545; SN 53 #114 (outline in Schleiermacher's hand) "Trost aus der Hoffnung, daß wir bei Christo sein warden." Betstunde 1887; Zimmer 67–68
John 18: ?	9.3.1828	Oculi	Hauptpredigt
*John 18:1–9	7.1.1827	1 Epiphany	Manuscript in de Gruyter archive: Sethe 1827a: 119
John 18:8–9	12.2.1826	Invocavit	Hauptpredigt; Manuscript in de Gruyter archive: Sethe 1826a: 84 [SN 66/1–12v song text excerpt for this Sunday]
*John 18:10–14	21.1.1827	3 Epiphany	Manuscript in de Gruyter archive: Sethe 1827a: 153
*John 18:15–27	18.2.1827	Exurge	Manuscript in de Gruyter archive: Sethe 1827a: 196
*John 18:28–32	4.3.1827	Invocavit	Manuscript in de Gruyter archive: Sethe 1827a: 223
*John 18:33–38	11.3.1827	Reminiscere	Hauptpredigt; Manuscript in de Gruyter archive: Sethe 1827a: 239
John 18:36–38	12.3.1826	Judica	Hauptpredigt; Manuscript in de Gruyter archive: Sethe 1826a: 122
*John 18:38—19:7	18.3.1827	Oculi	Frühpredigt
*John 19:8–16	25.3.1827	Laetare	Hauptpredigt
*John 19:16–24	1.4.1827	Judica	Frühpredigt

Biblical Text	Date Preached	Sunday in Church Year	Published Sermon Number, Sermon Title (if titled), Publication Data, or Manuscript Data
John 19:25–27	4.4.1797	Thursday before Palmarum	SN 52 #21 (outline in Schleiermacher's hand)
*John 19:25–29	8.4.1827	Palmarum	Hauptpredigt
John 19:26–27	25.3.1821	Oculi	Gedächtnispredigt für Prediger Heinstein
John 19:26–27	31.3.1833	Palmarum	
John 19:28–29	8.4.1821	Judica	P67; "Diese unbefangene Eingestandniß seines Bedürfnisses. Passions-predigt." 1835; SW II/4, 293–306
*John 19:30–42	13.4.1827	Karfreitag	Frühpredigt; ["634 Communicants—6 am" noted in daily diary]
John 19:30	25.3.1796	Charfreitag	P495; SN 51: 111–12 (outline in Schleiermacher's hand) "Das Zeugnis, welches sich Jesu selbst gab." Charfreitag. 1882; Zimmer 371–72
John 19:30	20.4.1810	Charfreitag	P339; "Wie der Herr mit Recht sagen konnte, dass er vollbracht habe. Am Charfreitage." 1836; SW II/7, 383–90
John 19:30	15.4.1821	Palmsonntag	P111; "Der lezte Blikk auf das Leben. Passionspredigt." 1834; SW II/2, 138–50
John 20: ?	18.4.1830	Quasimodo-geniti	Hauptpredigt

Biblical Text	Date Preached	Sunday in Church Year	Published Sermon Number, Sermon Title (if titled), Publication Data, or Manuscript Data
John 20: ?	25.4.1830	Misericordias Domini	Frühpredigt
John 20: ?	10.4.1831	Quasimodogeniti	Hauptpredigt
John 20:1–10	28.3.1796	2 Oster	SN 51: 114–15 (outline in Schleiermacher's hand)
*John 20:1–18	15.4.1827	Oster	Hauptpredigt
John 20:4ff	19.4.1795	Misericordias Domini	
John 20:17	25.5.1797	Himmelfahrt	P498; SN 52 (outline in Schleiermacher's hand) "Die Beruhigung desjenigen, der seinen Hingang so ansieht wie Christus." 1882; Zimmer, 374–75 (this transcription of the outline omits significant material in the manuscript)
John 20:17	11.4.1830	Oster	Hauptpredigt
*John 20:19	16.4.1827	Ostermontag	
John 20:19–23	12.4.1795	Quasimodogeniti	SN 51: 52–53 (outline in Schleiermacher's hand)
John 20:19–23	23.4.1797	Quasimodogeniti	(the same as 1795)
John 20:19–23	9.4.1820	Quasimodogeniti	

Biblical Text	Date Preached	Sunday in Church Year	Published Sermon Number, Sermon Title (if titled), Publication Data, or Manuscript Data
John 20:19	3.4.1796	Quasimodo-geniti	P497; SN 51:116–17 (outline in Schleiermacher's hand) "Ueber die Verheimlichung unsrer religiösen Ueberzeugungen." 1882; Zimmer 373–74
John 20:19ff	28.4.1811	Misericordias Domini	
John 20:19	1.1.1834	Neujahrstage	P233; "Der Inhalt des Grußes des Erlösers, Friede sei mit euch! In Beziehung auf unser ganzes mannigfaltiges Leben. Am Neujahrstage 1834." 1835; SW II/3, 752–64 English translation: Lawler, *Fifteen Sermons*, 258–77.
John 20:21	12.5.1833	5 Oster	(Rogate) P207; "Der Auftrag des Herrn an seine Jünger im Zusammenhang mit dem Wünsche, den er voranschickt. Am 5. Sonntage nach Ostern 1833." 1835; SW II/3, 563–73
John 20:21–23	1807 (before 6.4.1807)		"Uebereinstimmung mit dem Urteil Gottes." Referred to in Bauer, *patriotischer Prediger*, 44.
John 20:22–23	29.4.1821	Quasimodo-geniti	Hauptpredigt

Biblical Text	Date Preached	Sunday in Church Year	Published Sermon Number, Sermon Title (if titled), Publication Data, or Manuscript Data
John 20:24ff	19.4.1795		P581; "Wie glücklich diejenigen sind, die sich in den Besitz des Glaubens zu setzen wissen, den Jesus meinte." SN 51: 54–55 (outline in Schleiermacher's hand) Predigtentwurf am Sonntag Misericord. Dom. 1795 in Landsberg." 1909; Bauer, 104–109
John 20:24ff	11.5.1816		Vorbereitungspredigt vor Cantate; Manuscript in de Gruyter archive: transcription Ns Jonas 1816 f2
John 20:24–29	16.4.1820	Misericordias Domini	
*John 20:24–31	29.4.1827	Misericordias Domini	Frühpredigt
John 20:27	24.4.1831	Jubilate	Hauptpredigt
John 20:30–31	30.4.1826	Rogate	Hauptpredigt
John 21: ?	28.4.1822	Jubilate	Hauptpredigt
John 21:1–4	2.5.1830	Jubilate	Hauptpredigt
John 21:1–8	21.4.1833	Misericordias Domini	P205; (Daily diary cites this sermon as John 21:2f) "Wie die Jünger des Herrn zum Zurücksehen auf die Zeit, welche sie hinter sich halten, angeregtwurden. Am 2. Sonntage nach Ostern 1833." 1835; SW II/3, 537–49

Biblical Text	Date Preached	Sunday in Church Year	Published Sermon Number, Sermon Title (if titled), Publication Data, or Manuscript Data
*John 21:1–14	6.5.1827	Jubilate	Hauptpredigt
John 21:2–23(22)	12.4.1812	Misericordias Domini	P39; SN 92–105 (transcription not from Schleiermacher's hand) "Das Zusammensein der Jünger unter sich und mit dem Erlöser, als Vorbild unseres vertrauten Lebens mit unseren Freunden." 1834; SW II/1, 462–77
*John 21:15–19	13.5.1827	Cantate	Hauptpredigt
John 21:15	10.4.1796	Misericordias Domini	SN 51: 118–19 (outline in Schleiermacher's hand)
John 21:15	20.4.1800	Quasimodogeniti	P531; SN 53: 27 (outline in Schleiermacher's hand) "Wie übel wir thun, wenn wir bei unserm Bestreben, besser zu warden, davon ausgehen, besser warden zu wollen als andere." Sonntag (Werdersche Kirche—a Lutheran congregation). 1887; Zimmer 43–45
John 21:15	20.4.1800	Quasimodogeniti	P532; SN 53: 28 (outline in Schleiermacher's hand) "Daß man bei der Selbstprüfung nicht von Vergleichung mit andern ausgehen müsse." Sonntag, Nachmittag (Charité—Reformed chaplaincy) 1887; Zimmer 45–46

Biblical Text	Date Preached	Sunday in Church Year	Published Sermon Number, Sermon Title (if titled), Publication Data, or Manuscript Data
John 21:16	27.4.1823	Cantate	P70; Hauptpredigt "Ueber die Worte des Erlösers: Hast Du mich lieb? Predigt am Sonntage Cantate 1823 in der Dreifaltigkeitskirche." 1835; SW II/4, 143–56
John 21:16	9.5.1830	Cantate	Hauptpredigt
John 21:17–19	26.4.1795	Jubilate	SN 51: 56–57 (outline in Schleiermacher's hand)
John 21:17	19.5.1816	Rogate	Manuscript in de Gruyter archive: transcription Ns Jonas 1816 f6
John 21:18–19	1807 (before 6.4.1807)		"Fortschritte des Wortes Gottes."
John 21:18	27.5.1821	Rogate	Nachmittags
John 21:19ff	1.5.1831	Cantate	Hauptpredigt
*John 21:20–25	20.5.1827	Rogate	Hauptpredigt; "Schluss"
John 21:21–23	3.5.1795	Cantate	SN 51: 58–59 (outline in Schleiermacher's hand)
John 21:21–23	27.4.1800	Misericordias Domini	P536; SN 53 #186 (outline in Schleiermacher's hand) "Wie nachteilig es ist, in Kleinigkeiten eine große Bedeutung zu suchen." Sonntag, Nachmittag (Charitékirch e). 1887; Zimmer 50–51

Appendix B

Church Prayer from 1713

BERNHARD Schmidt quotes Schleiermacher describing his own practice in a letter to Joachim Christian Gass, saying: "After the sermon I take an excerpt, as I always used to do elsewhere, from the old 'church prayer' [from 1713] which was also taken up into the addendum to the liturgy."[1] Schmidt provides the entire text of this prayer from 1713 in his comparison of Schleiermacher's liturgical practice in 1829 with the content of the prescribed liturgy (*Agenda*) of 1829.[2] The rubrics accompanying the prayer indicate that it may be shortened in actual use.

> Almighty and eternal God, our gracious Father in Jesus Christ, we thank you with all our hearts that you have kindly sustained us in this temporal life until now and have by thy Gospel, of thy Son, let us be called to and prepared for eternal life, just as even now we are then able to hearken to thy holy word, in and quiet to our very end.
>
> Humbly we beseech thee, do thou continue to look upon us by thy grace, forgive us our sin and our transgression, and renew us in the spirit of our minds and hearts, that we may serve thee in holiness and righteousness, as is pleasing to thee. Sustain us by the preaching of thy word, together with a pure use of thy holy sacrament, and grant faithful shepherds and teachers to us and to those who succeed us. By thy might, guide and protect us from all temptations and leading astray, away from the power of godliness, that with one voice thy name may be hallowed therewith, as in the

1. Schmidt, *Lied—Kirchenmusik—Predigt*, 330 footnote and 325.
2. Ibid., 330–32. My translation.

entirety of Christendom so in this our land as well, that thy reign may increase, and that Satan's reign may be broken more and more.

In every sector, do thou favorably receive thy church, particularly the persecuted, and provide for it guardians and nurses in all sovereign authorities and regents. Especially, O God, in thy protection and grace may you be commended to all who are bound with us, Kaiser, king and princes, that they might promote all that addends to the general welfare and peace.

To the very end, O God, in your protection and grace may you be commended to all Christian potentates. Above all, may thy compassion loom large over our most treasured king and lord, over the regal princes and princesses and all who are related to the king's house and devoted to it. Do thou set them a long and healthy life for a constant blessing and Christian example to thy people for ever and ever. Especially willst thou, O Lord, impart our king to his governance and lend him a wise heart, thoughts worthy of a king, wholesome counsels, honest works, a strong arm, a courageous spirit, intelligent and faithful deliberation in times of war and peace, a triumphant army in war, loyal and obedient subjects, that in all godliness we may live a calm and peaceable life under his shield and protections for a long time to come. Take unto thy fatherly bosom all officers and soldiers, high and low, keep watch over the ins and outs of their journey, rule their hearts on each occasion, that they may diligently and dutifully live up to the oath they have carried out at such cost. Shelter them from illness and infectious disease and all other evils. Let thy fatherly love and caring be acknowledges in such a way that their service may redound to thy honor, for the protection of the church and of the fatherland, as also to their temporal and eternal welfare. We also commend to you all civil servants, high and low, who, both here and elsewhere, seek and promote what is best, especially for the king and the fatherland, as also a highly prudent counsel and judgment for this city.

Teach them all to comport themselves harmoniously therein, that law and justice may be rightly administered, and all that is of an unjust nature expunged, by their service.

Stand by them with thy fatherly assistance, that the sins and sighs of this land may diminish and thy blessings among us may increase.

O thou God of warring hosts, be with the kings army and its troops in all respects, lend them good fortune and victory, wherewith constantly to preserve a more just peace for all.

Loving God, do thou bless all territories of thy king, bless the Christian rearing of children, bless all decent handling of animals and all livelihood made on land or water. Help each person in one's need and have mercy on all who cry out to thee. Embrace us in thy love, and let that we should all serve for the best in this world. In thy grace, turn away from us all scourges, war, hunger, and times of scarcity, emergencies of fire and flood, pestilence and other contagions of humans or beasts, or whatever else we have deserved on account of our sins.

Do thou give the beneficial rains and let the fruits of the earth do well. May there be a Savior for all human beings, in particular of thy faithful people.

Thou, holy God, guard us in the face of sin and shame, and stay by us with thy good Spirit, that we may not forget thy blessing and draw thy proper punishment to us.

We recognize, O Lord, when by thy forbearance you spare us, that it is not our righteousness that moves thee to this, for we are unworthy servants before thee, but thy undeserved mercy alone. By that mercy may we be further blessed and may our hearts incline to love of our neighbor and compassion toward all who suffer distress, that we may never forget to do good to everyone, even our enemy, that we may demonstrate that we are thy children.

Guard us from a bad and hasty death, and by thy Spirit and grace make us ready, more and more for a blessed end. Above all, however, drive us from Satan and all his temptations, and strengthen us in our faith in your Son Jesus, that we may overcome all terror in the face of death.

When at that hour our ears can no longer hear, let thy Holy Spirit give witness to our spirit that we, as thy children and co-heirs with Christ, that with Jesus we will soon be with thee in paradise.

When our eyes too can no longer see, open our eyes of faith, that we may then see thy heaven open before us, and our Lord Jesus at his Father's right hand, that we too are to be where he is.

When our tongues as well can no longer speak, at that hour in particular let thy Spirit advocate for us with unutterable sighs, and each one know in one's heart how to call out: Abba, dear Father, into thy hands I commend my spirit.

So, grant us, faithful God, that we may live in awe of thee, die in thy grace, fare into thy peace, rest in the grave under thy shelter, rise again by thy power, and therein inherit the blessed hope: eternal life! For the sake of your beloved Son, Jesus Christ our Lord, to whom, with thee and the Holy Spirit, be all hail and praise, honor and glory, now and forever. Amen! and Amen!

Bibliography

A complete bibliography of published works by Schleiermacher can be found in:

Meding, Wichmann von. *Bibliographie der Schriften Schleiermachers*. Schleiermacher-Archiv 9. Berlin: de Gruyter, 1992.

In addition to the list in Meding, a complete listing of all published sermons by Schleiermacher can be found in:

Tice, Terrence N.. *Schleiermacher's Sermons: A Chronological Listing and Account*. Schleiermacher: Studies and Translations 15. Lewiston, NY: Mellen, 1997.

For a record of all of the secondary literature on any aspect of Schleiermacher see the serial bibliography still being updated on a periodic basis by Terrence N. Tice in *New Athenaeum/Neues Athenaeum*. Lewiston, NY: Mellen. Installments published to date:

Tice, Terrence N. *Schleiermacher Bibliography*. Princeton Pamphlets 12. Princeton: Princeton Theological Seminary, 1966.

———. *Schleiermacher Bibliography (1784–1984) Updating and Commentary*. Princeton Pamphlets 101. Princeton: Princeton Theological Seminary, 1985.

———. "Schleiermacher Bibliography: Update 1987" *New Athenaeum/Neues Athenaeum*. 1 (1989) 280–350.

———. "Schleiermacher Bibliography: Update 1990" *New Athenaeum/Neues Athenaeum*. 2 (1991) 131–63.

———. "Schleiermacher Bibliography: Update 1994" *New Athenaeum/Neues Athenaeum*. 4 (1995) 139–94.

Such an extensive bibliographic record makes it necessary in this list to include only the works cited. I have, however, included manuscripts that I have examined but not cited because no published listing of manuscripts is as yet available and these items might otherwise be unknown to the reader.

1. Works by Schleiermacher

A. Published

Page numbers in the footnotes are from the first German edition given when two are listed. These page numbers also appear at the margin of the corresponding KGA editions.

Bauer, Johannes. *Schleiermacher als Patriotischer Prediger*. Giessen: Töpelmann, 1908.

———. *Ungedruckte Predigten Schleiermachers aus den Jahren 1820–1828*. Leipzig: Heinsius, 1909.

DeVries, Dawn, trans.. *Servant of the Word: Selected Sermons of Friedrich Schleiermacher*. Philadelphia: Fortress, 1987.

Jonas, Ludwig and Wilhelm Dilthey, et.al., eds. *Aus Schleiermacher's Leben: In Briefen*. 4 vols. Berlin: Reimer, 1861.

Lawler, Edwina, trans.. *Fifteen Sermons of Friedrich Schleiermacher Delivered to Celebrate the Beginning of a New Year.* Schleiermacher Studies and Translations 23. Lewiston, NY: Mellen, 2003.

Rachold, Jan, editor. *Friedrich Schleiermacher—eine Briefauswahl.* Frankfurt am Main: Peter Lang, 1995.

Schleiermacher, Friedrich D.E. "An die Mitglieder beider zur Dreifaltigkeitskirche gehörigen Gemeinden." Berlin: Reimer, 6 Dezember 1820. Also "An die Mitglieder beider zur Dreifaltigkeitskirche gehörenden Gemeinden (1820)." In *Kirchenpolitische Schriften*, edited by Günter Meckenstock and Hans-Friedrich Traulsen, 203–10. Kritische Gesamtausgabe I.9. Berlin: de Gruyter, 2000.

———. *Der christliche Glaube: nach den Grundsätzen der evangelischen Kirche im Zusammenhange dargestellt (1821/22)*. Edited by Hermann Peiter. Kritische Gesamtausgabe I.7, 3 vols.. Berlin: de Gruyter, 1980–1984.

———. *Der christliche Glaube: nach den Grundsätzen der evangelischen Kirche im zusammenhange Dargestellt Zweite Auflage (1830/31).* Seventh edition. Edited by Martin Redeker. 2 vols. Berlin: de Gruyter, 1960. Also *Der christliche Glaube: nach den Grundsätzen der evangelischen Kirche im Zusammenhange dargestellt Zweite Auflage (1830/31),* edited by Rolf Schäfer. Kritische Gesamtausgabe I.13, 2 vols.. Berlin: de Gruyter, 2003. Translation of second German Edition by H.R. Mackintosh and J.S. Stewart. *The Christian Faith*. Philadelphia: Fortress, 1928.

———. *Einleitung ins neue Testament*. Edited by G. Wolde. Sämmtliche Werke I/8. Berlin: Reimer, 1845.

———. *Hermeneutik*. Second Edition. Edited by Heinz Kimmerle. Heidelberg: C. Winter, 1974. Translation of second edition by James Duke and Jack Forstman. *Hermeneutics*. Missoula, MT: Scholars Press, 1977.

———. *Kurze Darstellung des Theologischen Studiums zum Behuf Einleitender Vorlesungen*. Third critical edition. Edited by Heinrich Scholz. 1910. Reprinted Darmstadt: Wissenschaftliche Buchgesellschaft, 1977. Also "Kurze Darstellung des theologischen Studiums." In *Schriften und Entwürfe*, edited by Dirk Schmid, 317–446. Kritische Gesamtausgabe I.6. Berlin: de Gruyter, 1998. Translation of the 1811 and 1830 editions by Terrence N. Tice. *Brief Outline of Theology as a Field of Study*. Schleiermacher Studies and Translations 1. Lewiston, NY: Mellen, 1990.

———. *Das Leben Jesu. Vorlesungen an der Universität zu Berlin im Jahr 1832.* Edited by K.A. Rütenik. Sämmtliche Werke I/6. Berlin: Reimer, 1864. Translated by S. Maclean

Gilmour. Edited by Jack C. Verheyden. *The Life of Jesus*. Philadelphia: Fortress, 1975.

———. *Die praktische Theologie nach den Grundsäzen der evangelischen Kirche in Zusammenhange dargestellt*. Edited by Jacob Frerichs. Sämmtliche Werke I/13. Berlin: Reimer, 1850.

———. *Predigten*. Sämmtliche Werke II/1. Berlin: Reimer, 1834.

———. *Predigten*. Sämmtliche Werke II/2. Berlin: Reimer, 1834.

———. *Predigten*. Sämmtliche Werke II/3. Berlin: Reimer, 1835.

———. *Predigten*. Sämmtliche Werke II/4. Berlin: Reimer, 1844.

———. *Predigten in den Jahren 1789 bis 1810 gehalten*. Edited by Ad. Sydow. Sämmtliche Werke II/7. Berlin: Reimer, 1836.

———. *Predigten. Homilien über das Evangelium des Johannes, in den Jahren 1823 und 1824 gesprochen*. Edited by Ad. Sydow. Sämmtliche Werke II/8. Berlin: Reimer, 1837.

———. *Predigten. Homilien über das Evangelium des Johannes, in den Jahren 1825 und 1826 gesprochen*. Edited by Ad. Sydow. Sämmtliche Werke II/9. Berlin: Reimer, 1847.

———. *Sendschreiben über seine Glaubenslehre an Lücke*. Edited by Hermann Mulert. Giessen: Töpelmann, 1908. Also "Über die Glaubenslehre. Zwei Sendschreiben an Lücke (1829)." In *Theologisch-dogmatsiche Abhandlungen und Gelegenheiten*, edited by Hans-Friedrich Traulsen and Martin Ohst, 307–94. Kritische Gesamtausgabe I.10. Berlin: de Gruyter, 1990. Translated by James Duke and Francis Fiorenza. *On the Glaubenslehre: Two Letters to Dr. Lücke*. American Academy of Religion Texts and Translations Series 3. Chico, CA: Scholars Press, 1981.

———. *Ueber die neue Liturgie für die Hof-und Garnison-Gemeinde zu Potsdam und für die Garnisonkirche in Berlin*. Berlin: Realschulbuchhandlung, 1816. Also "Über de neue Liturgie für die Hof-und Garnison-Gemeinde zu Potsdam und für die Garnisonkirche in Berlin." In *Kirchenpolitische Schriften*, edited by Günter Meckenstock and Hans-Friedrich Traulsen, 79–105. Kritische Gesamtausgabe I.9. Berlin: de Gruyter, 2000.

———. *Ueber die Religion: Reden an die Gebildeten unter ihren Verächtern*. Reprint of first edition. Edited by Hans-Joachim Rothert. Hamburg: Felix Meiner, 1958. Also *Über die Religion (2.-)4. Auflage, Monologen (2.-) 4. Auglage,* edited by Günter Meckenstock, 1–321. Kritische Gesamtausgabe I.12. Berlin: de Gruyter, 1995. Translated by Richard Crouter. *On Religion: Speeches to its cultured despisers*. First Edition. Cambridge: Cambridge University Press, 1988.

———. *Ueber die Schriften des Lukas*. 1817. Sämmtliche Werke I/2. Berlin: Reimer, 1836. Also "Über die Schriften des Lukas ein kritscher Versuch. Erster Theil." In *Exegetische Schriften*, edited by Hermann Patsch and Dirk Schmid, 1–180. Kritische Gesamtausgabe I.8. Berlin: de Gruyter, 2001. Translated by Connop Thrilwall. *Luke: A Critical Study*. Edited by Terrence N. Tice. Lewiston, NY: Mellen, 1993.

———. *Vorlesungen über die Lehre vom Staat*. Edited by Walter Jaeschke. Kritische Gesamtausgabe II.8. Berlin: de Gruyter, 1998.

Seidel, Dietrich and Terrence N. Tice, trans. *The Christian Household: A Sermonic Treatise*. Schleiermacher Studies and Translations 3. Lewiston, NY: Mellen, 1991.

Wilson, Mary, trans.. *Selected Sermons of Schleiermacher*. London: Hodder & Stoughton, 1890. Reprinted, Eugene, OR: Wipf and Stock, 2004.

Zimmer, Friedrich. *Predigtentwürfe aus dem Jahre 1800*. Gotha: n.p., 1887.

———. "Predigtenentwürfe aus Friedrich Schleiermachers erster Amtsthätigkeit." *Zeitschrift für praktische Theologie*. 4 (1882) 281–90, 369–78.

B. Manuscripts

This listing of manuscripts by no means includes all of the sermon manuscripts available in these two archives. This listing identifies only those on Johannine texts in the Berlin-Brandenburg Akademie der Wissenschaften Archiv. The de Gruyter Verlagshaus Archiv collection is presently being catalogued by the Schleiermacher Forschungstelle in Kiel.

Jonas Nachschrift 1816 f6 in de Gruyter publishing house archive, Berlin.

Jonas Nachschrift 1816 f14 in de Gruyter publishing house archive, Berlin.

Pishon Nachschrift on John 1:14 (unnumbered) corrected by Schleiermacher in de Gruyter publishing house archive, Berlin.

Schleiermacher Nachlass 8 "Zum Johannes Evangelium" undated. In Akademie der Wissenschaften, Berlin. Verse by verse commentary on entire text.

Schleiermacher Nachlass 46 "Den Evangelien" undated. In Akademie der Wissenschaften, Berlin. Lecture notes.

Schleiermacher Nachlass 51 [Predigt Entwürfe Landsberg] in Akademie der Wissenschaften, Berlin.

Schleiermacher Nachlass 52 [Predigt Entwürfe] in Akademie der Wissenschaften, Berlin.

Schleiermacher Nachlass 53 [Predigt Entwürfe] in Akademie der Wissenschaften, Berlin.

Schleiermacher Nachlass 69 "Zum Leben Christi" undated. In Akademie der Wissenschaften, Berlin. Extended lecture notes.

Schleiermacher Nachlass 70 "Leben Jesu 1832" in Akademie der Wissenschaften, Berlin. Extended lecture notes.

Schleiermacher Nachlass 71 [Entwürf] "1832" in Akademie der Wissenschaften, Berlin.

Schleiermacher Nachlass 227 "Zum Armen Wesen" in Akademie der Wissenschaften, Berlin. Noted by Nowak, "Schleiermacher als Prediger," 403 (see below). (This is the only manuscript I have not personally seen.)

Schleiermacher Nachlass 597/ 1,2,3 [Nachschriften in three different hands] in Akademie der Wissenschaften, Berlin.

Schleiermacher Nachlass 608/ 1,2,3,4 [Nachschriften perhaps all by one person] in Akademie der Wissenschaften, Berlin.

Sethe 1826a "Nachschriften" notebook in de Gruyter publishing house archive, Berlin.

Sethe 1826b "Nachschriften" notebook in de Gruyter publishing house archive, Berlin.

Sethe 1827a "Nachschriften" notebook in de Gruyter publishing house archive, Berlin.

2. Other Works Cited

Albrecht, Christoph. *Schleiermachers Liturgik: Theorie und Praxis des Gottesdienstes bei Schleiermacher und ihre geistesgeschichtlichen Zusammenhänge*. Göttingen: Vandenhoeck & Ruprecht, 1963.

Barth, Karl. *Die Theologie Schleiermachers*. Gesammtausgabe V.2. Zürich: Theologischer Verlag, 1978.

———. *The Theology of Schleiermacher: Lectures at Göttingen, Winter Semester of 1923/24*. Edited by Dietrich Ritschl and translated by Geoffrey W. Bromiley. Grand Rapids: Eerdmans, 1982.

Bauer, Johannes. *Schleiermacher als patriotischer Prediger: ein Beitrag zur Geschichte der nationalen Erhebung vor hundert Jahren*. Giessen: Töpelmann, 1908.

Baur, Ferdinand Christian. *Die christliche Lehre von der Dreieinigkeit und Menschwerdung Gottes in ihrer geschichtlichen Entwicklung: Dritter Theil, Die neuere Geschichte des Dogma, von der Reformation bis in die neueste Zeit.* Tübingen: Osiander, 1843.

Beske, Hans and Ernst Handke, editors. *Landsberg an der Warthe 1257–1945–1976 Stadt und Land im Umbruch der Zeiten.* Bielefeld: Ernst und Werner Gieseking, 1976.

Birkner, Hans-Joachim. *Theologie und Philosophie: Einführung in Probleme der Schleiermacher-Interpretation.* Munchen: Kaiser, 1974.

Blackwell, Albert L. "Martensen's 'Bekenntnis zu Schleiermacher' (1833). New Light on It's Historical Setting and A New Musical Setting of Its Text." In *Schleiermacher und die Wissenschaftliche Kultur des Christentums*, edited by Günter Meckenstock and Joachim Ringleben. Berlin: de Gruyter, 1991, 3–12.

Bretschneider, Karl Gottlieb. *Probabilia de Evangelii et Epistolarum Joannis, Apostoli, Indole et Origine: Eruditorum Judiciis.* Leipzig: Barthii, 1820.

Brunner, Emil. *Die Mystik und das Wort.* Tübingen: Mohr, 1924.

Clark, W. Royce. "The Fourth Gospel and Christology in Modern Dogmatic and Systematic Theology." In *Johannine Studies: Essays in Honor of Frank Pack*, edited by James E. Priest, 17–35. Malibu, CA: Pepperdine University Press, 1989.

Creed, James Martin. *The Divinity of Jesus Christ: A study in the history of Christian doctrine since Kant.* London: Cambridge University Press, 1938.

Crouter, Richard. "Friedrich Schleiermacher: A Critical Edition, New Work, and Perspectives." *Religious Studies Review.* 18 (1992) 20–27.

Demps, Laurenz, et.al. *Geschichte Berlins von den Anfängen bis 1945.* Berlin: Dietz, 1987.

DeVries, Dawn. *Jesus Christ in the Preaching of Calvin and Schleiermacher.* Louisville, KY: Westminster John Knox, 1996.

———, trans. *Servant of the Word: Selected Sermons of Friedrich Schleiermacher.* Philadelphia: Fortress, 1987.

Dilthey, Wilhelm. *Leben Schleiermachers.* 2 vols. 1870. Gesammelte Schriften 13. Reprint Göttingen: Vandenhoeck & Ruprecht, 1970.

Foley, Peter. *Friedrich Schleiermacher's* Essay on a Theory of Sociable Behavior *(1799): A Contextual Interpretation.* Lewiston, NY: Mellen, 2006.

Frei, Hans W. *Types of Christian Theology.* Edited by George Hunsinger and William Placher. New Haven: Yale University Press, 1992.

Gerdes, Hayo. *Der geschichtliche biblische Jesus oder der Christus der Philosophe: Erwägungen zur Christologie Kierkegaards, Hegels und Schleiermachers.* Berlin: Verlag der Spur, 1974.

———. "Anmerkungen zur Christologie der Glaubenslehre Schleiermachers." *Neue Zeitschrift für systematische Theologie und Religionsphilosophie.* 25 (1983) 112–25.

Gerrish, Brian A. *A Prince of the Church: Schleiermacher and the Beginnings of Modern Theology.* Philadelphia: Fortress, 1984.

———. "UBI THEOLOGIA, IBI ECCLESIA? Schleiermacher, Troeltsch, and the Prospect for an Academic Theology." In *Religious Studies, Theological Studies and the University-Divinity School*, edited by Joseph Mitsuo Kitagawa. Atlanta: Scholars Press, 1992.

Gräb, Wilhelm. "Predigt als kommunikativer Akt: Einige Bermerkungen zu Schleiermachers Theorie religiöser Mitteilung." In *Internationaler Schleiermacher-Kongress Berlin 1984*, edited by Kurt-Victor Selge, Part 2.643–59. Schleiermacher-Archiv 1. Berlin: de Gruyter, 1985.

Griesbach, Jo.Jac. *Novum Testamentum Graece.* 2nd Edition. 2 vols. Halle: Curtii, 1796.

Hase, Karl. *Geschichte Jesu.* Leipzig: Breitkopf und Härtel, 1876.

Herz, Henriette. *Berliner Salon: Erinnerungen und Partraits*. Frankfurt am Main: Ullstein, 1984.

Herzberg, Gustav Frd. *Geschichte der Stadt Halle an der Saale während des 18. und 19. Jahrhunderts*. Halle: Buchhandlung des Waisenhauses, 1893.

Hildebrandt, Irma. *Zwischen Suppenküche und Salon: achtzehn Berlinerinnen*. Köln: Diederichs, 1987.

Hirsch, Emanuel. *Geschichte der neuern evangelischen Theologie*. 5 vols. Gütersloh: Bertelsmann, 1954.

———. *Schleiermachers Christusglaube: Drei Studien*. Gütersloh: Mohn, 1968.

Hoffbauer, Johann Christoph. *Geschichte der Universität zu Halle bis zum Jahre 1805*. 1805. Reprint Aalen: Scientia, 1981.

Jaeckel, Gerhard. *Die Charité: Die Geschichte eines Weltzentrums der Medizin*. 1963. Reprint Bayreuth: Hestia, 1986.

Jørgensen, Theodor. "Predigt als Selbstdarstellung." In *Schleiermacher und die Wissenschaftliche Kultur des Christentums*, edited by Günter Meckenstock. Berlin: de Gruyter, 1991.

Jung, Kurt Gerhard. *Der Erlösungsbegriff in den frühen Predigten Friedrich Daniel Ernst Schleiermachers*. PhD. Diss. Berlin, 1971.

Junker, Maureen. *Das Urbild des Gottesbewusstseins: zur Entwicklung der Religionstheorie und Christologie Schleiermachers von der ersten zur zweiten Auflage der Glaubenslehre*. Schleiermacher-Archiv 8. Berlin: de Gruyter, 1990.

Keck, Leander E. "Introduction." In *The Christ of Faith and the Jesus of History: A Critique of Schleiermacher's Life of Jesus*, by David Friedrich Strauss. Philadelphia: Fortress, 1977

Kümmel, Werner Georg. *Das Neue Testament: Geschichte der Erforschung seiner Probleme*. Munchen: Alber Freiburg, 1958.

Lange, Dietz. *Historischer Jesus oder mythischer Christus: Untersuchungen zu dem Gegensatz zwischen Friedrich Schleiermacher und David Friedrich Strauss*. Gütersloh: Mohn, 1975.

Lücke, Friedrich. *Commentar über die Schriften des Evangelisten Johannes*. 3 vols. Bonn: Weber, 1820–1825.

———. "Erinnerungen an Dr. Friedrich Schleiermacher." *Theologische Studien und Kritiken* (1834) 745–813.

Mariña, Jacqueline. "Christology and anthropology in Friedrich Schleiermacher." In *The Cambridge Companion to Friedrich Schleiermacher*, edited by Jacqueline Mariña, 151–70. Cambridge: Cambridge University Press, 2005.

Mayer, Rudolf. "Die Form der Predigt Schleiermachers." *Dienet einander! Monatschrift für praktische Theologie und Religionsunterricht der Schule* 25 (Sept. 1917) 161–73.

Meckenstock, Günter. *Schleiermachers Bibliothek: Bearbeitung des faksimilierten Rauchschen Auktionskatalogs und der Hauptbücher des Verlages Reimer*. Schleiermacher-Archiv 10. Berlin: de Gruyter, 1993.

Meding, Wichmann von. *Bibliographie der Schriften Schleiermachers nebst einer Zusammenstellung und Datierung seiner gedruckten Predigten*. Schleiermacher-Archiv 9. Berlin: de Gruyter, 1992.

Meier-Dörken, Christoph. *Die Theologie der frühen Predigten Schleiermachers*. Berlin: de Gruyter, 1988.

———. "Zum Verhältnis zwischen Schleiermachers Predigten und seinen Romantischen Schriften." In *Internationaler Schleiermacher-Kongress Berlin 1984*, edited by Kurt-Victor Selge, Part 2:661–679. Schleiermacher-Archiv 1. Berlin: de Gruyter, 1985.

Melzer, Friso. "Zu der Frage nach dem dogmatischen Gehalt von Schleiermachers Predigten." *Theologische Studien und Kritiken* 102 (1930) 282–424.

———. "Christus in der Predigt Schleiermachers." *Theologische Studien und Kritiken* 104 (1932) 54–83.

Moretto, Giovanni. "Angezogen un belehrt von Gott: Der Johannismus in Schleiermachers <<Reden über Religion>>." *Theologische Zeitschrift* 37 (1981) 267–91.

Niebuhr, Richard R. "Schleiermacher on Language and Feeling." *Theology Today* 17 (July 1960) 150–67.

———. *Schleiermacher on Christ and Religion*. London: SCM Press, 1964.

Nowak, Kurt. *Schleiermacher: Leben, Werk und Wirkung*. Göttingen: Vandenhoeck & Ruprecht, 2001.

———. "Schleiermacher als Prediger am Charité-Krankenhaus in Berlin (1796–1802)." *Theologische Zeitschrift* 41 (1985): 391–411.

Perrin, Norman. *Rediscovering the Teaching of Jesus*. London: SCM, 1967.

Reich, Andreas. *Friedrich Schleiermacher als Pfarrer an der Berliner Dreifaltigkeitskirche 1809–1834*. Schleiermacher Archiv 12. Berlin: de Gruyter, 1992.

Ribbe, Wolfgang, editor. *Geschichte Berlins: Von der Frühgeschichte bis zur Industrialisierung*. 2 vols. Munchen: Beck, 1987.

Robinson, John A.T. *The Priority of John*. Edited by J.F.Coakley. London: SCM, 1985.

Roy, D. Henri. "Das unmittlebare Erleben der Gegenwart Christi in der Erfahrung des Christen nach Schleiermachers Predigten." *Monatschrift für Pastoraltheologie* 22.516 (1926): 115–23.

Schmidt, Bernhard. *Lied—Kirchenmusik—Predigt im Festgottesdienst Friedrich Schleiermachers: Zur Rekonstruktion seiner liturgischen Praxis*. Schleiermacher-Archiv 20. Berlin: de Gruyter, 2002.

Schweitzer, Albert. *The Quest of the Historical Jesus: A Critical Study of Its Progress from Reimarus to Wrede*. Translated by W. Montgomery. London: Black, 1910

Seifert, Paul. *Die Theologie des jungen Schleiermachers*. Gütersloh: Mohn, 1960.

Sheehan, James J. *German History 1770–1866*. Oxford: Clarendon, 1989.

Strauss, David Friedrich. *Das Leben Jesu, kritisch bearbeitet*. Tübingen: Osiander, 1835. Translated by Marian Evans. *The Life of Jesus Critically Examined*. 2 vols. New York: Blanchard, 1856.

———. *The Christ of Faith and the Jesus of History: A Critique of Schleiermacher's Life of Jesus*. Translated by Leander E. Keck. Philadelphia: Fortress, 1977.

Tice, Terrence N. *Schleiermacher*. Nashville, TN: Abingdon, 2006.

———. "Themes in Schleiermacher's Early Theology." In *Papers of the Schleiermacher Seminar*, American Academy of Religion 1989 Annual Meeting, Chicago, edited by Terrence N. Tice, 1–26. Ann Arbor: University of Michigan, 1989.

Trillhaas, Wolfgang. *Schleiermachers Predigt*. 1933. Reprint, Berlin: de Gruyter, 1975.

———. "Der Berliner Prediger." In *Friedrich Schleiermacher 1768–1834: Theologe-Philosoph-Pädagoge*, edited by Dietz Lange. Göttingen: Vandenhoeck & Ruprecht, 1985, 9–23.

Urner, Hans. "Schleiermacher als Prediger." In *Friedrich Schleiermacher Predigten*, edited by Hans Urner. Göttingen: Vandenhoeck und Ruprecht, 1969, 9–20.

Vial, Theodore. "Schleiermacher and the state." In *The Cambridge Companion to Friedrich Schleiermacher*, edited by Jacqueline Mariña, 269–85. Cambridge: Cambridge University Press, 2005.

Virmond, Wolfgang. "Liederblätter—ein unbekanntes Periodikum Schleiermachers Zugleich ein Beitrag zur Vorgeschichte und Entstehung des Berliner Gesangbuchs von 1829." In *Schleiermacher in Context,* 275–93. Schleiermacher Studies and Translations 6. Lewiston, NY: Mellen, 1991.

Vollack, Manfred. *Hinterpommern in Farbe: Von der Ostsee zur Grenzmark*. Mannheim: Kraft, 1986.

Weisweiler, Hilger. *Schleiermachers Arbeiten zum Neuen Testament.* Bonn: Rheinische Friedrich-Wilhelms-Universität, 1972.

Wilhelmy, Petra. *Der Berliner Salon im 19. Jahrhundert: 1780–1914*. Historical Commission of Berlin 73. Berlin: de Gruyter, 1989.

Wolfes, Matthias. *Öffentlichkeit und Bürgergesellschaft: Friedrich Schleiermachers politische Wirksamkeit.* 2 vols. Schleiermacher Studien 1. Berlin: de Gruyter, 2004.

Names and Places Index

Subjects and Concepts Index

R

W